TOP **10**
VENICE

Top 10 Venice Highlights

The Top 10 of Everything

CONTENTS

Venice Area by Area

Streetsmart

Within each Top 10 list in this book, no hierarchy of quality or popularity is implied. All 10 are, in the editor's opinion, of roughly equal merit.

Title page, front cover and spine *The iconic Rialto Bridge on the Grand Canal*
Back cover, clockwise from top left *Tiramisù, a classic Italian dessert; central dome of the Basilica di San Marco; view over Venice rooftops; Rialto Bridge; colourful boats and buildings line a canal*

The information in this DK Eyewitness Top 10 Travel Guide is checked regularly. Every effort has been made to ensure that this book is as up to date as possible at the time of going to press. Some details, however, such as telephone numbers, opening hours, prices, gallery hanging arrangements and travel information are liable to change. The publishers cannot accept responsibility for any consequences arising from the use of this book, nor for any material on third-party websites, and cannot guarantee that any website address in this book will be a suitable source of travel information. We value the views and suggestions of our readers very highly. Please write to: Publisher, DK Eyewitness Travel Guides, Dorling Kindersley, 80 Strand, London WC2R 0RL, UK, or email travelguides@dk.com

Welcome to
Venice

Gliding gondolas. Glorious sunsets over the lagoon. Spritz *aperitivos*. Black cuttlefish-ink pasta. Renaissance *palazzi*. Gorgeous Carnival masks. A time warp. And no cars; not one. It doesn't matter how many times you've been, a visit to Venice is always as memorable as it is romantic. Navigating the canal-filled city is easy with this Eyewitness Top 10 Venice guide.

There's nothing like Venice anywhere else in the world. Join the crowds thronging **Piazza San Marco** and wonder at the glittering **Basilica**. Relax at the outdoor cafés, drinking in the atmosphere while sipping a cappuccino, or ride a water-bus plying the canals.

Whether you come for a couple of days or a whole week, our *Top 10 Venice* guide is invaluable, with its carefully selected listings that bring together the best the city has to offer. Explore the labyrinthine **Doge's Palace**, have a drink in buzzing **Campo Santa Margherita**, hunt for a costume for the annual **Carnival**, shop at top craft stores and fashion boutiques, or travel to the atmospheric islands of **Murano** and **Torcello**.

Succinct descriptions explain how Venice developed as and where it did, with the help of notable figures such as Marco Polo and Vivaldi. Insider tips abound, along with curious facts that you won't find in any other guide. Your questions will be answered: Is Venice still sinking? Do people often fall in the water?

Whether you're coming for a weekend or a week, our Top 10 guide brings together the best of everything the city can offer. There are tips throughout, from seeking out what's free to avoiding the crowds, plus ten easy-to-follow itineraries, designed to help you visit a clutch of sights in a short space of time. Add inspiring photography and detailed maps, and you've got the essential pocket-sized travel companion. **Enjoy the book, and enjoy Venice.**

Clockwise from top: **Giudecca; lion statue in Piazza San Marco; Basilica San Marco mosaic; Grand Canal; Carnival mask; gondolas with San Giorgio Maggiore in the background; Burano**

Exploring Venice

Venice is a sightseeing paradise for people of all ages. To make the most of a holiday and see the best the city has to offer, here are some time-efficient ideas for both two- and four-day stays.

The Grand Canal cuts a meandering path through Venice and offers a delightful perspective from the water.

Two Days in Venice

Day ❶

MORNING

Start off at the marvellous **Basilica di San Marco** *(see pp12–15)* before wandering around the **Piazza San Marco** *(see pp20–21)*. The Campanile tower gives a superb view over the city.

AFTERNOON

A visit to the **Doge's Palace** *(see pp16–19)* can be followed by a laid-back ride on a *vaporetto* all the way up the glorious **Grand Canal** *(see pp24–5)* past many elegant *palazzi* and under the Accademia and Rialto bridges.

Day ❷

MORNING

Begin with Venetian art at the **Accademia Galleries** *(see pp30–31)* before strolling through to **Campo Santa Margherita** *(see pp38–9)* for a bite to eat.

AFTERNOON

It's a short walk to the Venetian Gothic masterpiece **Santa Maria Gloriosa dei Frari** *(see pp32–3)* and, from there, on to the lovely Campo San Polo square with its great neighbourhood feel.

Four Days in Venice

Day ❶

MORNING

The natural place to start any visit is the magnificent main square, **Piazza San Marco** *(see pp20–21)*. Visit the panoramic Campanile or the Torre dell'Orologio (booking essential), then have a coffee at the legendary – but expensive – **Caffè Florian** *(see p21)*. Refreshed, head into the **Basilica di San Marco** *(see pp12–15)* to wonder at the ancient mosaics.

AFTERNOON

After lunch, take time to explore the **Doge's Palace** *(see pp16–19)*, once the powerhouse of the Maritime Republic. Don't miss the Bridge of Sighs and the dank prisons.

The impressive Doge's Palace dominates the waterfront leading to Piazza San Marco

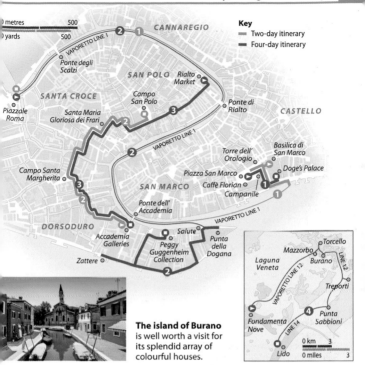

The island of Burano is well worth a visit for its splendid array of colourful houses.

Day ❷
MORNING
Catch a *vaporetto* at Piazzale Roma or the railway station for the spectacular trip along the **Grand Canal** *(see pp24–5)*, passing beneath Rialto Bridge. Alight at Salute to visit the **Punta della Dogana** *(see p98)*.
AFTERNOON
After lunch on the sun-blessed **Zattere** *(see p101)*, backtrack to see the impressive **Peggy Guggenheim Collection** *(see pp40–41)*.

Day ❸
MORNING
Make an early start to enjoy the best of **The Rialto**, a fish and produce market, which is open mostly in the morning *(see pp34–5)*. It's then just a short walk to the church of **Santa Maria Gloriosa dei Frari** *(see pp32–3)*, a masterpiece of Venetian Gothic architecture.

AFTERNOON
Campo Santa Margherita *(see pp38–9)* is a bustling square with inviting cafés and restaurants ideal for lunch. After you have eaten, proceed to the **Accademia Galleries** *(see pp30–31)* for an overview of Venetian painting through the centuries.

Day ❹
MORNING
Take a leisurely ferry trip over the Northern Lagoon to the island of **Torcello** *(see pp36–7)*, where you can admire the Byzantine mosaics in the Basilica. Then continue to neighbouring **Burano** *(see p121)* or **Mazzorbo** *(see p117)* for lunch.
AFTERNOON
Pick up a ferry to take you cruising via Treporti and **Punta Sabbioni** to the **Lido** *(see pp123–4)* for a trip to the beach. Afterwards, head back to Venice proper.

Top 10 Venice Highlights

**Basilica di Santa Maria della Salute
viewed from Ponte dell'Accademia**

🔟 Venice Highlights

The uniquely romantic city of Venice was built entirely on water and has managed to survive into the 21st century without cars. Narrow alleyways and canals pass between sumptuous palaces and magnificent churches, colourful neighbourhood markets and quiet backwaters, unchanged for centuries. Few cities possess such an awe-inspiring line-up of sights for visitors.

Basilica di San Marco ①

Venice's fairy-tale cathedral is distinctly Byzantine, and its façade and interior have been embellished with resplendent mosaics and works of art through the ages *(see pp12–15)*.

② Doge's Palace

This was the powerhouse of the city's rulers for nearly 900 years. Passing through the maze of gilded rooms gives visitors a fascinating insight into the extravagant lifestyle that so often accompanied state affairs *(see pp16–19)*.

③ Piazza San Marco

Elegance and opulence sit side by side in what Napoleon named "the finest drawing room in Europe". This magnificent square is adorned with monuments that bear testimony to Venice's history *(see pp20–23)*.

④ Grand Canal

The city's majestic water-course swarms with all manner of boats, while its embankments boast a dazzling succession of palaces dating back as early as the 13th century *(see pp24–7)*.

Accademia Galleries

This unsurpassed collection of Venetian paintings includes masterpieces by Titian, Bellini and Giorgione. It is a must, not only for art lovers *(see pp30–31)*.

Santa Maria Gloriosa dei Frari

A Gothic interior with grandiose works of art lies in store behind this church's brick façade *(see pp32–3)*.

The Rialto

A fresh produce market has enlivened this quayside since medieval times and is arguably still the best market in the world *(see pp34–5)*.

CAMPO SAN STAE

PO S.
COMO
L'ORIO

CAMPO SAN CASSIANO

CAMPO DEI SANTI APOSTOLI

CAMPO S. GIACOMO DI RIALTO

SAN POLO

CAMPO SAN POLO

RIVA DEL VIN

Ponte di Rialto

Canal Grande

CASTELLO

CAMPO SAN LUCA

CALLE DEI FABBRI

CAMPO MANIN

SAN MARCO

CAMPO S. ANGELO

CAMPO S. FANTIN

FREZZERIA

PO SAN AMUELE

CAMPO S. STEFANO

CAMPO S. MAURIZIO

C. LARGA XXII MARZO

CPO SAN MOISE

Ponte dell' Accademia

Canal Grande

CAMPO DELLA SALUTE

| 0 metres | 300 |
| 0 yards | 300 |

Torcello

Escape the crowds in the city with a ferry ride over the vast expanse of the lagoon to this peaceful, lush island, the site of Venice's original settlement *(see pp36–7)*.

Campo Santa Margherita

Thanks to its market stalls and outdoor cafés, this lovely square is always bustling with life. An added bonus are the many architectural styles *(see pp38–9)*.

Peggy Guggenheim Collection

Italy's leading museum for 20th-century European and American art is housed in a palace on the Grand Canal *(see pp40–41)*.

PEGGY GUGGENHEIM COLLECTION

TOP 10 ⭐ Basilica di San Marco

The breathtaking Byzantine basilica dominating Piazza San Marco *(see pp20–23)* was constructed in such ornate fashion for two reasons: as an embodiment of the Venetian Republic's power and as a fitting resting place for St Mark. Serving as the doges' chapel, it was the site of coronations, funerals and processions, all gloriously framed by more than 4,000 sq m (43,000 sq ft) of mosaics, eastern treasures and 500 columns, some dating back to the 3rd century.

Western Façade ①

A marvellous succession of domes, columns, arches and spires, **(right)** interspersed with marble statues, screens and glittering mosaics, greets tourists in Piazza San Marco. The northernmost arch houses 13th-century mosaics that depict the basilica itself. Other mosaics are 17th- and 18th-century copies.

② Atrium Mosaics

These glorious mosaics **(left)** of precious gold-leaf over glass tiles were created in the Byzantine tradition by expert craftsmen, and give detailed accounts of the Old Testament. The 13th-century cupola's concentric circles recount 24 episodes from Genesis, including the Creation and Adam and Eve.

③ Flooring

The elaborate paving is a mosaic masterpiece of multicoloured stones on uneven levels, evocative of the sea. Intricate geometrical designs sit alongside animal shapes.

Basilica Floorplan

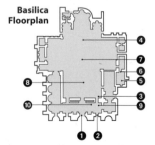

Pala d'Oro ④

The dazzling jewel-encrusted gold screen **(right)** was commissioned in Constantinople in 976 but frequently added to at later dates. It has 250 panels bearing 1,927 authentic gems and cloisonné plaques.

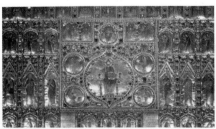

BUILDING THE BASILICA

Construction first began in 829, but it was burned down in 976, in a revolt. The building dates from 1071 and has a Greek cross lay-out capped by five domes. The architect is shown over the central portal, biting his fingers in frustration. The basilica became the city cathedral in 1807.

Ascension Dome (7)

The central dome has a spectacular array of early 13th-century mosaics, depicting the New Testament. *Christ in Glory* is shown above depictions of the Virtues **(right)**.

(8) Pentecost Dome

What is probably the first dome of the basilica to be adorned with mosaics depicts the Descent of the Holy Ghost, seen as a flame over the heads of the 12 apostles.

(9) Basilica Museum

Here you'll find the famed quartet of horses crafted from bronze and covered in gold. Booty from the Fourth Crusade, these restored Graeco-Roman equine figures originally graced the Hippodrome in Constantinople.

Loggia dei Cavalli (10)

Replicas of the horses **(right)**, now in the museum, stand on this balcony over-looking Piazza San Marco. Visitors can also see clutches of columns, whose dimensions and decorative styles indicate their origins.

The Tetrarchs (5)

The inspiration for these red porphyry rock figures is unknown. They probably represent the four emperors of the eastern and western Roman empires **(right)**. The statue was pillaged from Constantinople during the Fourth Crusade in 1204.

(6) Treasury

The basilica's glittering riches include precious chalices of rock crystal enamelled by medieval silver- and goldsmiths and reliquaries from Venice's eastern conquests, including parts of the True Cross.

NEED TO KNOW

MAP Q5 ▪ Piazza San Marco ▪ 041 270 83 11 ▪ www.basilicasanmarco.it

Guided visits: book on www.alata.it

Basilica: Open mid-Apr–Oct: 9:30am–5pm Mon–Sat, 2–5pm Sun & pub hols; Nov–mid-Apr: 9:30am–5pm Mon–Sat, 2–4:30pm Sun & pub hols

Pala d'Oro, treasury and Loggia dei Cavalli: Open mid-Apr–Oct: 9:35am–5pm; Nov–mid-Apr: 9:45am–4:45pm Mon–Sat, 2–4:30pm Sun & pub hols; adm Pala d'Oro €2; treasury €3

Museum: Open mid-Apr–Oct: 9:35am–4:45pm daily; adm €5

▪ Pre-book tickets online to beat the queues.

▪ Visit at dusk, when the setting sun lights up the façade.

▪ Take binoculars to examine the mosaics, but you must leave backpacks in the luggage room.

Basilica Architectural Features

1 Galleries
The airy catwalks over the body of the basilica reflect the eastern tradition of segregation in worship, as they were exclusively for women. They are closed to visitors.

2 Stone Wall-Slabs
Brick-faced until the 1100s, the walls of the basilica were then covered with stone slabs from the East, sliced lengthways to produce a kaleidoscopic effect.

3 Romanesque Stone Carvings
The exquisite semicircular stone carvings over the central doorway were executed between 1235 and 1265 and still bear traces of their original colouring.

4 The "Victory Bringer"
This revered Byzantine icon is given pride of place in the Madonna of Nicopeia Chapel. Rumoured to have been executed by St Luke, it was carried into battle for its miraculous powers.

5 Baptistry
Aglow with 14th-century mosaic scenes of the life of St John, this is also home to the tomb of Italian architect Jacopo Sansovino *(see p55)*. Open for prayer only.

Basilica Floorplan

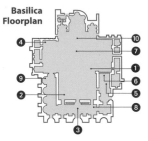

6 Zen Chapel
The ornate decoration in this chapel was executed for the funeral of its namesake, Cardinal Zen, in 1521, in recognition of his gifts to the state. Open for prayer only.

The ornate Iconostasis

7 Iconostasis
This elaborate screen separates the worship area of the chancel from the nave. Atop its eight columns are Gothic-style statues of the Virgin and the apostles, sculpted by the Dalle Masegne brothers in 1394.

8 Byzantine Pierced Screens
Influenced by eastern architecture, delicate geometrical designs and lattice-work stone screens are featured on all three façades, in the atrium and loggia.

9 Porta dei Fiori
This doorway on the northern façade bears a 13th-century nativity scene surrounded by Moorish arches.

10 Altar Columns
Four finely carved alabaster and marble columns support a canopy at the altar, beneath which lies the body of St Mark.

Font in the Baptistry

ST MARK, PATRON SAINT OF VENICE

Although the well-loved saint of Byzantium St Theodore had been appointed protector of Venice by the Byzantine emperor, the fledgling republic felt in need of a saint of its own. According to legend, in AD 828, two adroit Venetian merchants filched the body of St Mark from a monastery in Alexandria, transporting it under layers of pork fat to conceal it from Muslim guards. The welcome in Venice was triumphant, and the story was recounted in countless paintings and mosaics. The remains, however, were mislaid for years, until an arm miraculously broke through a column in 1094 (marked by a small cross, left of the Altar of the Sacrament) in answer to a prayer. St Mark now rests in peace beneath the basilica's main altar. The ubiquitous winged lion representing St Mark could be found throughout the republic as the trademark of Venetian dominion: it is

often shown with two paws in the sea and two on land, to symbolize the geography of Venice.

The Miracle of the Relic of the True Cross on the Rialto Bridge (1494) by Vittore Carpaccio

TOP 10
VENICE RELICS

1 Milk of the Virgin Mary, Basilica Treasury (see p13)

2 Blood of Christ, Basilica Treasury

3 Nail from the True Cross, Chiesa di San Pantalon (see p49)

4 Thorn from Christ's crown, Basilica Treasury

5 Body of St Mark, Basilica San Marco (see pp12–13)

6 Body of St Lucy, Chiesa di San Geremia

7 Three rocks used to stone St Stephen to death, Basilica Treasury

8 Skull of St John the Baptist, Basilica Treasury

9 Leg of St George, Basilica Treasury

10 Foot of St Catherine of Siena, Santi Giovanni e Paolo (see p48)

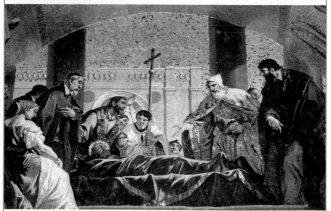

This mosaic in Basilica San Marco depicts the veneration of the body of St Mark by the Doge.

TOP 10 ⭐ Doge's Palace

A magnificent combination of Byzantine, Gothic and Renaissance architecture, the Palazzo Ducale (Doge's Palace) was the official residence of the 120 doges who ruled Venice from 697 to 1797. A fortress-like structure stood here in the 9th century, to be replaced by the elegant Gothic version seen today, despite a string of fires in the 1500s. Artists such as Titian, Tintoretto and Bellini vied with each other to embellish the palace with painting and sculpture, not to mention architects Antonio Rizzo and Pietro Lombardo, the latter responsible for the western façade.

1 Façade
Elegant twin façades face the piazzetta and the quayside. Pink-and-cream stonework and a loggia stand above an arcade of columns with 36 sculpted Istrian stone capitals **(above)**.

2 Sala del Senato
Senate members met in this lavish hall **(below)** to debate war, foreign affairs and trade with the Doge. Time was measured by two clocks – one with a 24-hour face, the other with zodiac signs.

3 Armoury
This is a gripping, if spine-chilling, collection of beautifully crafted firearms, ceremonial weapons and suits of armour **(left)** from Asia and the West. Among the war trophies is a Turkish standard brought back from the Battle of Lepanto (1571).

4 Prisons
A fascinating maze of cells is linked by corridors and staircases on both sides of the canal. One of the most famous inmates, Casanova *(see p50)*, made a dramatic escape across the roof in 1756. The "new prisons" were in use until the 1940s and feature poignant graffiti by internees.

Scala d'Oro 7

The magnificent Golden Staircase **(right)**, so-called for its Classical stucco decorations in 24-carat gold-leaf framing frescoes, led guests of honour to the second floor. Designed by Sansovino *(see p57)*, it was later completed by Scarpagnino in 1559.

5 Bridge of Sighs

One of the world's most famous bridges **(above)**, the Ponte dei Sospiri is an early 17th-century Baroque structure that crosses to the palace prisons. It reputedly caused the condemned to "sigh" at their last glimpse of sky and sea.

6 Sala dello Scudo

Enormous globes **(below)** and painted wall maps showing the known world in 1762 make this room a must. The map of Eastern Asia traces Marco Polo's travels to China, complete with camels, rhinos and the mythical Uncharted Lands of the People Eaters.

8 Porta della Carta

The palace's main entrance (now the visitors' exit) has a beautifully sculpted 1438 portal by the Bon family. The name "paper door" arose because edicts were posted here.

9 Sala del Maggior Consiglio

The Great Council Chamber **(left)** is lined with canvases of Venetian victories and a cornice frieze of 76 doges – a black curtain represents traitor Marin Falier *(see p19)*.

10 Doge's Apartments

The communicating rooms of the Doge's living quarters include rich brocades, triumphal friezes, gilded ceilings and works of art.

NEED TO KNOW

MAP R5

- Piazza San Marco
- 041 240 52 11 ■ www. visitmuve.it

Open Apr–Oct: 8:30am–7pm daily (to 11pm Fri & Sat); Nov–Mar: 8:30am–5:30pm daily (last admission 60 min before closing time); closed 1 Jan, 25 Dec

Adm €20 (includes entry to the Museo Correr Complex)

Secret Itineraries Tour: 848 08 20 00 (advance booking essential at palace, by phone or online); 9:55am, 10:45am & 11:35am daily in English; tickets: €20 (€14 concessions)

■ A quiet, modern café in the former stables on the ground floor serves snacks and drinks.

■ The Museo dell'Opera, near the ticket office, houses many of the original 14th-century façade capitals – those outside are mostly 19th-century copies.

Doge's Palace Art and Architecture

Veronese's *Rape of Europa*

1 Rape of Europa
Veronese's allegorical work (1580) in the AntiCollegio shows Europa sitting on a bull, alias Jove, who is nuzzling her foot.

2 Paradise
Possibly the world's largest oil painting (1588–90), *Paradise* by Jacopo and Domenico Tintoretto is said to contain 800 figures (Sala del Maggior Consiglio).

3 Arcade Capital
Proclaimed the "most beautiful in Europe" by art critic John Ruskin, this eight-sided carved capital on the southwest corner shows the zodiac signs and planets in imaginative detail.

4 The Triumph of Venice
Dominating the Sala del Senato is Tintoretto's glorious work of propaganda (1580–84), showing allegorical and mythological figures proffering fruits of the sea to Venice.

5 Central Balcony
This magnificent early 15th-century stone terrace, embellished with columns, spires and a host of saints, opens off the Sala del Maggior Consiglio with a breathtaking view of the lagoon.

6 Arco Foscari
This triumphal archway of pink-and-cream stone layers leading to the Giants' Staircase was commissioned by Doge Foscari in 1438.

7 Wellheads
Elaborate 16th-century wellheads were constructed to drain water from the gutters to the palace's central courtyard.

8 Drunkenness of Noah
A powerful sculpture from the early 15th century adorns the façade's southeast corner. Noah, inebriated and half-naked before his sons, is intended to portray the weakness of man.

Drunkenness of Noah

9 Coronation of the Virgin
The faded but inspired remains of Guariento's fresco, discovered beneath Tintoretto's *Paradise*, are housed in a side room, with panels explaining the restoration techniques.

10 Giants' Staircase
So named for its two colossal statues of Mars and Neptune, which were sculpted by Sansovino in 1567 as symbols of Venice's power. Visiting dignitaries would ascend the marble-lined stairs to the palace.

Giants' Staircase

THE EXTENT OF THE VENETIAN REPUBLIC

Doge Gradenigo with the Venetian fleet at the siege of Chioggia, 1379

In its earliest days, Venice was little more than a huddle of islands in the middle of a shallow marshy lagoon, settled by a band of refugees from the Veneto region. Yet over the centuries it developed into a mighty republic reaching south to the Mediterranean and north to the Alps, based on the concept of trade. Salt was stored in massive warehouses, there were dealings in exotic spices and wondrous fabrics from the East, crusades were organized and fitted out here, and relics procured. Its main population probably never exceeded 160,000, however, well beyond its walled port towns, which stretched down the Dalmatian coast, were far-flung outposts such as Crete and Cyprus. These dominions protected key passages in commerce with the Arabic countries. Westward across the Po plain, Venice's influence took in Treviso, Vicenza and Verona, extending all the way to Bergamo on the outskirts of Milan and the mighty Visconti dynasty.

The Republic's gaining of maritime power is celebrated in *The Victorious Return of Doge Andrea Contarini after Triumph in Chioggia* by Paolo Veronese (1525–88).

**TOP 10
EVENTS IN THE
VENETIAN REPUBLIC**

1 Venice founded on 25 April (St Mark's Day, AD 421)

2 First doge, Paoluccio Anafesto, elected (697)

3 St Mark's body brought to Venice (828)

4 Ruthless siege of Constantinople during the Fourth Crusade under Doge Enrico Dandolo (1204)

5 Venice loses 60 per cent of its population to the Black Death (1348)

6 Doge Marin Falier decapitated for conspiracy (1355)

7 Genoese defeated at Battle of Chioggia, leaving Venice to reign over the Adriatic and Mediterranean (1381)

8 Victory over Turks at Battle of Lepanto (1571)

9 After 25 years of war, Crete is lost to the Turks (1669)

10 Napoleon invades the Veneto, bringing about the fall of the Venetian Republic (1797)

TOP 10 ★ Piazza San Marco

Long the political and religious heart of Venice, it's hard to believe Piazza San Marco was once just a monastery garden crossed by a stream. The glittering basilica and Doge's Palace command the east side of the square, while other stately buildings along its borders have been the backdrop for magnificent processions. The western end was remodelled by Napoleon, who wished to construct a royal palace here. Today the piazza continues to bustle, with a museum complex *(see p22)*, cafés and costumed Carnival crowds.

1 Basilica di San Marco
See pp12–15.

2 Doge's Palace
See pp16–19.

3 Torre dell'Orologio

A marvel to behold, the imposing and impressive Renaissance-style clock tower is topped by two bronze Moors **(left)** hammering out the hours on the upper terrace. At Epiphany and Ascension there is an hourly procession of clockwork Magi that are led by an angel. According to legend, the craftsmen were subsequently blinded to prevent them repeating the work.

The Piazzetta and the Palace

NEED TO KNOW
MAP Q5

Campanile: Open 1–15 Apr: 9am–5:30pm; mid-Apr–Oct: 8:30am–9pm; Nov–Mar: 9:30am–5:30pm; book guided tours on www.venetoinside.com; Adm €8

Torre dell'Orologio: 041 427 308 92 (from abroad); 848 082 000 (from Italy); Guided tours: 10am & 11am Mon–Wed, 2pm & 3pm Thu–Sun. Adm €12.

Museo Correr Complex: Open 10am–7pm; Nov–Mar: 10am–5pm (last admission 1 hour before closing). Adm €20 (includes Doge's Palace)

■ The best time to appreciate the beauty of the square is early morning, when only the city sweepers are here.

4 Campanile

Incomparable views of the city and lagoon can be had by taking the elevator to the top of this 98-m (323-ft) bell tower **(right)**. It was masterfully rebuilt to its 16th-century design following its clamorous collapse in 1902.

5 Piazzetta
Once an inlet for boats and witness to the arrival of distinguished visitors during the Republic's heyday, this now fully paved mini square fronts the lagoon.

6 Column of San Marco

This is one of two granite columns erected in 1172 by Nicolò Barattieri **(left)**; the other symbolizes San Teodoro. Public executions were held here.

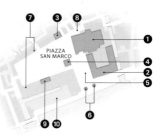

Plan of Piazza San Marco

VENICE'S BELLS

Booming through the city, the five bells in the Campanile have been employed to mark Venice's rhythms for centuries. The Maleficio bell was sounded to announce an execution, the Nona rang at midday, the Trottiera spurred on the nobles' horses for assemblies in the Doge's Palace and the Mezza Terza was used to indicate that the Senate was in session. The Marangona bell is still sounded to mark midnight.

7 Procuratie Vecchie and Nuove

The Procurators, who were responsible for state administration, lived in these elegant 15th-century buildings **(below)**.

8 Piazzetta dei Leoncini

This is the site of a former vegetable market, where a pair of small lions *(leoncini)* carved from red Verona stone **(right)** have been crouching since 1722.

9 Caffè Florian

Reputedly Europe's first coffee house *(see p83)*, the premises still retain their original 1720 wood-panelling, marble-topped tables and gilt-framed mirrors.

10 Giardinetti Reali

These shady public gardens, created during the Napoleonic era, took the place of boatyards and grain stores, situated just behind the panoramic waterfront.

Museo Correr Complex

1 Biblioteca Marciana Ceiling

The ceiling vault of the opulent reading room *(sale monumentali)*, inside the Libreria Sansoviniana, collapsed in 1545 and architect Sansovino imprisoned – he was released to complete the job at his own expense. Titian selected artists for the decorations; Veronese was awarded a gold chain for the best work.

2 Libreria Sansoviniana Staircase

Bedecked with gilt and stucco decorations by Alessandro Vittoria, the 16th-century stair-case leads from a monumental entrance on the piazza to the halls of the old library.

Canova's statue of Orpheus

3 Veneziano Paintings

This prolific Byzantine artist is featured in the Pinacoteca's Room 25 (part of Museo Correr), with glowing two-dimensional religious portraits (1290–1302).

Correr Ballroom

4 Correr Ballroom

This showy Neo-Classical creation was built for Napoleon. It is now used for exhibitions.

5 Two Venetian Ladies

Carpaccio's masterpiece of well-dressed ladies (1500–10) is in Room 38 of the Museo Correr. It was first thought to depict courtesans because of the ladies' décolléte dresses, but the women are, in fact, awaiting their menfolk's return from hunting.

6 Canova Statues

In the Museo Correr, works by Antonio Canova (1767–1822), foremost sculptor of his time, include his acclaimed statues of Orpheus and Eurydice.

7 Map of Venice

Pride of place in Room 32 of the Museo Correr goes to Jacopo de' Barbari's prospective map-layout of Venice (1497–1500), which was painstakingly engraved on six pear-wood panels.

8 Bellini Room

Works by the talented Bellini family are on display in Room 36 of the Pinacoteca: the poignant *Dead Christ Supported by Two Angels* (1453–5) by the best known, Giovanni; head of the family Jacopo's *Crucifixion* (1450); and son Gentile's portrait of *Doge Giovanni Mocenigo* (1475).

9 Narwhal Tusk

Once prized as the horn of the fabled unicorn, this 1.6-m- (5-ft-) long tusk from the rare whale has been superbly carved with Jesse's and Jesus's family tree (Room 40 in Museo Correr).

10 Crafts and Guilds

Wooden sandals 60-cm (24-inches) high, inlaid with mother-of-pearl, illustrate the stiff demands put upon followers of 15th–17th-century fashion (Room 48).

ACQUA ALTA FLOODING

Acqua Alta ("high water") has long been disruptive to the city between October and March. As warning sirens fill the air, people drag out their waterproof boots, shopkeepers rush to put up protective barriers and street-sweepers lay out duck-boards in low-lying spots. Venice and its lagoon are subject to the tides of the Adriatic Sea but flood levels are caused by the coincidence of low atmospheric pressure, strong sirocco winds from the south and natural high tides due to moon phases. Piazza San Marco is among the most vulnerable spots. The flood gates designed for the Lido sea entrances are held by many experts to be both useless and harmful to the lagoon. However, there are plans for an elaborate drainage system on the piazza, dredging canals and raising paving levels.

Bullfight in St Mark's Square **by Canaletto and Giovanni Battista Cimaroli**

Piazza San Marco is located in a vulnerable position on the edge of the lagoon and has been flooded by high tides throughout its history.

TOP 10
HISTORIC EVENTS IN PIAZZA SAN MARCO

1 Foundations of Doge's Palace laid (AD 814)

2 Construction of basilica started (828)

3 First bullfight held (1162)

4 Square paved with brick, herringbone-style (1267)

5 Square paved with volcanic trachyte blocks (1722–35)

6 Napoleon demolishes San Geminiano church to make way for Ala Napoleonica (1810)

7 Campanile crumbles to the ground (1902)

8 Record flood 1.94 m (6.4 ft) above sea level (4 November 1966)

9 Pink Floyd rock concert attracts 100,000 (1989)

10 Campanile stormed by Venetian separatists (1997)

TOP 10 ⭐ Grand Canal

Venice's majestic "highway", the Canal Grande, is only one of the 177 canals flowing through the city, but at some 4 km (2.5 miles) in length, 30–70 m (98–230 ft) in width and averaging 4.5 m (15 ft) in depth, it certainly earns its name. Snaking its way through the city with a double curve, its banks are lined with exquisite palaces, while on its waters colourful flotillas of gondolas, ferries, taxi launches, high-speed police boats and barges groaning under fresh produce provide endless fascination. In 1818, when the water was cleaner, Lord Byron swam all the way down the Grand Canal from the Lido.

1 Fondaco dei Turchi
With an exotic air and its round arches, this Veneto-Byzantine building (1225) **(above)** was the Turkish trade centre for 200 years. It is now the Natural History Museum *(see p62)*.

2 Ca' Pesaro
This colossal Baroque palace *(see p57)*, decorated with diamond-point ashlar work, was the final creation of architect Longhena. Home to the city's modern art collections, it is beautifully floodlit at night.

The view towards Santa Maria della Salute

3 Rialto Bridge
One of the city's most familiar sights, the striking 28-m- (92-ft-) wide, 8-m- (26-ft-) high Istrian stone Ponte di Rialto **(below)** dates from 1588.

4 Riva del Vin
A sunny quayside with a string of open-air restaurants, this is one of the few accessible banks of the Grand Canal. Barrels of wine *(vino)* used to be off-loaded here, hence the name.

5 Ca' Rezzonico
The finest feature of this imposing palace is its grandiose staircase **(right)**. Today it is a museum of 18th-century Venice.

7 Ca' Dario

With an ornamental Renaissance façade studded with multicoloured stone medallions, this lopsided palace is supposedly cursed due to a number of misfortunes that have overtaken its various owners.

6 Accademia Bridge

The lovely wooden Ponte dell'Accademia **(above)**, built in 1932 by the engineer Miozzi, was intended as a temporary measure until a more substantial structure was designed, but it is now a permanent fixture. It affords stunning views of the Grand Canal.

8 Santa Maria della Salute

Longhena's 17th-century masterpiece of sculpted whorls beneath a towering dome **(right)**, this church *(see p48)* commemorates the end of a devastating plague in the city.

WAVE DAMAGE

Damage to buildings caused by wash has worsened of late with the rise in motor-propelled craft. Waves provoked by all boats eat into foundations of buildings on the water's edge, as well as making life harder for the gondoliers. Speed limits aim to curb this: 7 kmph (4.5 mph) for private craft and 11 kmph (7 mph) for waterbuses on the Grand Canal. Narrower canals mean 5 kmph (3 mph), while 20 kmph (12.5 mph) is the lagoon maximum.

NEED TO KNOW

The Grand Canal runs from Piazzale Roma, the bus terminal and car park area, to Piazza San Marco. It is easily navigable courtesy of ferries Nos. 1 (all stops) and 2 (main stops only)

■ Take the *vaporetto* line No. 1 to enjoy the best views of the sights along the canal.

■ To beat the crowds, start out from Piazzale Roma heading towards San Marco in the late afternoon or evening, or take the reverse direction in the morning.

9 Punta della Dogana

The figure of Fortune **(right)** stands atop the erstwhile customs house, now an arts centre *(see p98)*, and doubles as a weather vane. This is where the Grand Canal joins St Mark's Basin.

10 Harry's Bar

The legendary watering hole *(see p71)* of Ernest Hemingway is where the Bellini *aperitivo* was invented. Opened in 1931 by Arrigo Cipriani, it was named after the American who funded it.

Watercraft of Venice

Typical Venetian gondola

1 Gondola

These are most often seen transporting tourists around the canals. A larger version *(traghetto)* is also used for the cross-canal ferry *(see p139)*, while the smaller *gondolino* is a slender racing craft.

2 Vaporetto

Strictly speaking, this is the capacious rounded waterbus, now also seen in an "ecological" electric model. A slimmer *motoscafo* serves the outer runs and narrow canals with relatively low bridges.

3 Sandolo

A slim, lightweight boat perfectly suited to hunting and fishing in the shallow waters of the lagoon, not to mention racing. Painted black, these "imitation gondolas" can deceive tourists on the back canals.

4 Topo

The most common barge for transporting goods around the canals, the *topo* can be seen loaded with everything from washing machines to demijohns, often with a live dog "figurehead" on the prow.

5 Sanpierota

This flat-bottomed rowing boat is named after the inhabitants of San Pietro in Volta *(see p125)* in the southern lagoon. Once used for transporting fish to Venice, nowadays it is fitted with an outboard motor and photogenic oblique sail.

6 Bragozzo

With its gently rounded prow and stern, this brightly coloured sailing boat was traditionally used for fishing by the inhabitants of Chioggia *(see p125)*.

7 Fire Boat

From their station near Ca' Foscari, the red launches are called both to deal with fires and to rescue submerged obstacles and crumbling façades.

8 Garbage Vessel

The city's hefty waste-collecting AMAV barges trundle over the lagoon with the day's rubbish, in addition to carrying out environmental monitoring.

Ambulance launch

9 Ambulance and Police Launches

These modern craft attract plenty of attention as they roar down the canals – only the emergency categories are allowed to disregard the city's speed limits.

10 Car Ferry

These giants convey all manner of motor vehicles from the Tronchetto to the Lido.

VENICE'S GONDOLAS

The quintessential sleek Venetian gondola has been plying the city's canals since as early as the 11th century, although it did not take on its present graceful form until the late 1400s. Compared to a mere 405 gondolas on the waterways today, as many as 10,000 were in use in the late 19th century: bridges were once few and far between and gondolas acted as ferries between one island and another, a custom that continues to this day across the Grand Canal by the *traghetti*. A handful of gondola yards still construct the boats as well as carry out repairs, such as San Trovaso in Dorsoduro *(see p98)*. It's a costly and complex craft – eight different types of wood are needed for a total of 280 pieces to make the asymmetrical craft, 11 m (36 ft) in length and 1.42 m (4.5 ft) in width, at a cost approaching €25,000.

TOP 10
GONDOLA FEATURES

1 *Forcola* (rowlock)
2 *Ferro* (prow bracket)
3 *Hippocampus* (side ornament)
4 Night lamp
5 Bronze stern decoration
6 Ribbed oar
7 *Felze* (cabin)
8 Gondolier's foot rest
9 Gondolier's striped shirt
10 Gondolier's straw hat

The iron bracket (ferro) on the prow weighs 30 kg (66 lb) to offset the weight of the rower, and adds to the more than 350-kg (770-lb) weight of the gondola. Originally painted in bright colours, the black gondolas that you see today were decreed by the Senate to prevent excessive shows of wealth.

Gondola repair yard

TOP 10 ⭐ Accademia Galleries

A dazzling collection of masterpieces spanning the full development of Venetian art from Byzantine to Renaissance, Baroque and Rococo, the Gallerie dell'Accademia is Venice's equivalent of the Uffizi in Florence. Giovanni Battista Piazzetta started the collection in 1750 to serve as models for the art school; in 1807 it was boosted by Napoleon with the addition of works from suppressed churches. The same year the collection moved to its present premises, occupying three former religious establishments: the 12th–15th-century Scuola Grande di Santa Maria della Carità and its adjoining church, and a 12th-century monastery remodelled by Palladio in the 1500s. In the 1940s, architect Carlo Scarpa *(see p55)* modernized the interior spaces.

San Giobbe Altarpiece ①

Giovanni Bellini's inspirational altarpiece **(right)** (Room 2) was painted in 1487 for the Church of San Giobbe. It is regarded as one of the finest examples of Sacra Conversazione, which was central to 15th-century Venetian art. The presence of St Sebastian and St Giobbe beside the Virgin suggests the aftermath of plague, while angel musicians pay homage to San Giobbe, patron saint of music.

② The Tempest

This enigmatic 1506 portrayal of a woman suckling her child **(left)** is by Giorgione (Room 23). The overall impression is of the figures and the dream-like, stormy landscape blended into one whole.

③ Supper in the House of Levi

The forceful canvas by Veronese (1573) occupies an entire wall of Room 10 and caused controversy in its time. The church authorities, who commissioned it as "The Last Supper", were angered by the inclusion of "dogs, buffoons, drunken Germans, dwarfs and other such absurdities" – so Veronese changed the title.

④ Pietà

Titian's last work (1576) is unfinished but it is also considered his best (Room 10), imbued as it is with golden light and a piercing sense of anguish.

Previous pages Gondolas on the Grand Canal

5 Meeting and Departure of the Betrothed Ursula and Ereo

Part of Carpaccio's magnificent narrative cycle (1495) about a Breton princess and an English prince can be seen in Room 21.

Gallery Floorplan

6 Procession in St Mark's Square

Part of Gentile Bellini's spectacular cycle (1496) of the St Mark's Day procession in 1444 **(above)** can be seen in Room 20.

7 Madonna dell'Arancio

This exquisite work (1496–8) by Cima da Conegliano, painted for a Murano Franciscan church, is enlivened with partridges and plant life (Room 2).

NEED TO KNOW

MAP L6 ■ Campo della Carità, Dorsoduro 1050 ■ 041 522 22 47 ■ www.gallerieaccademia.it

Open 8.15am–7:15pm daily (to 2pm Mon; last admission 45 minutes before closing); closed 1 Jan, 1 May, 25 Dec

Adm €12

■ The galleries are currently undergoing extensive expansion, so the floorplan may differ from that shown here until the work is completed in mid-2019.

Gallery Guide

The vast gallery is organized in chronological order for the most part and the rooms, labelled with roman numerals, are equipped with explanatory cards in English. The Quadreria corridor is filled with masterpieces.

8 Coronation of the Virgin

This resplendent polyptych (1350) by Venice's leading 14th-century artist, Paolo Veneziano, is the first work in Room 1. Flanking the stunning Byzantine-inspired central piece are events depicted from the life of Christ.

9 Portrait of a Gentleman

Lorenzo Lotto's sombre image of a melancholic man of means in his study (1528) **(above)** may be a self-portrait (Room 7). Lotto was known for works of psychological insight.

10 Lion of St Mark with Saints John the Baptist, John the Evangelist, Mary Magdalene and Jerome

This marvellous canvas (in Room 23) by Cima di Conegliano depicts a winged lion flanked by four saints.

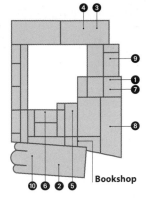

🔟 ⭐ Santa Maria Gloriosa dei Frari

A masterpiece of Venetian Gothic ecclesiastical architecture, this cavernous 15th-century church for Franciscan friars took more than 100 years to complete, along with its "brother" SS Giovanni e Paolo *(see p48)*, and a further 26 years for the consecration of the main altar. A wonderful series of art treasures is held within the deceptively gloomy interior, which is almost 100-m (330-ft) long and 50-m (165-ft) across, from priceless canvases by Titian and Bellini to tombs of doges and artists such as Canova.

1 Assumption of the Virgin

Titian's glowing 1518 depiction of the triumphant ascent of Mary **(left)** shows her robed in crimson accompanied by a semicircle of saints, while the 12 apostles are left gesticulating in wonderment below. This brilliant canvas on the high altar is the inevitable focus of the church.

Santa Maria Gloriosa dei Frari

2 Rood Screen

This beautiful screen, which divides the worship area and nave is carved in a blend of Renaissance and Gothic styles by Pietro Lombardo and Bartolomeo Bon (1475). It is also decorated with marble figures **(right)**.

5 Campanile

The robust 14th-century bell tower set into the church's left transept is the second tallest in Venice.

3 Choir Stalls

Unique for Venice, the original three tiers of 124 friars' seats deserve close examination for their inlaid woodwork. Crafted by Marco Cozzi in 1468, they demonstrate the influence of northern European styles.

4 Madonna Enthroned with Saints

Tucked away in the sacristy, and still in its original engraved frame, is another delight for Bellini fans (1488). "It seems painted with molten gems," wrote Henry James of the triptych.

Canova's Mausoleum 6

This colossal monument **(right)**, based on Canova's Neo-Classical design for Titian's tomb, which was never built, was a tribute by the sculptor's followers in 1822.

8 Monument to Doge Francesco Foscari

This is a fine Renaissance tribute to the man responsible for Venice's mainland expansion. Foscari was the subject of Lord Byron's *The Two Foscari*, which was turned into an opera by Verdi.

Statue of John the Baptist 9

The inspirational wood statue of John the Baptist from 1450 **(right)**, which was created especially for the church by artist Donatello (1386–1466), stands in the Florentine chapel. The striking emaciated carved figure is renowned for being particularly lifelike.

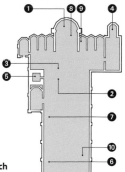

10 Monument to Titian

Titian was afforded special authorization for burial here after his death during the 1576 plague, although this sturdy mausoleum was not built for another 300 years.

Church Floorplan

7 Mausoleum of Doge Giovanni Pesaro

The monsters and black marble figures supporting the sarcophagus of this macabre Baroque monument prompted art critic John Ruskin to write "it seems impossible for false taste and base feeling to sink lower".

NEED TO KNOW

MAP L3 ■ Campo dei Frari, San Polo ■ 041 275 04 62 ■ www.chorus venezia.org

Open 9am–6pm Mon–Sat, 1–6pm Sun (last admission 30 min before closing time); closed 1 Jan, Easter, 15 Aug, 25 Dec

Adm €3; Chorus Pass €12 (includes admission to 18 churches)

■ There are some great cafés and eateries in Campo dei Frari.

■ Enjoy the nativity scene with lighting effects and moving figures at Christmas.

TOP 10 ⭐ The Rialto

The commercial hub of Venice, centred on the Rialto Bridge (see p58), is as bustling today as it has always been – records tell of markets here since 1097. The area is also the city's historical heart and took its name from Rivoaltus, the high consolidated terrain that guaranteed early settlers flood-free premises. Most buildings, however, date from the 16th century, because a fire swept through Rialto in 1514. During Carnival the stall-holders don medieval costume to vie with each other for custom and only the new awnings and electronic cash registers hint at the modern world.

① Fresh Produce Market
The market here is a treat for the senses, with artistic piles of luscious peaches and cherries, thorny artichokes and red chicory from Treviso. Fruit, vegetables and fish are strictly seasonal **(above)**.

Rialto market alongside the Grand Canal

③ San Giacomo di Rialto
The oldest church in Venice claims to have a foundation set by a pious carpenter in the 5th century, although the present building is medieval. The Gothic portico and 24-hour clock are well worth a look.

④ Public Rostrum
New laws and names of criminals were announced atop this porphyry column **(right)**, supported by a stone figure known as *il gobbo* (hunchback).

② Pescheria
Writhing eels, huge swordfish, soft-shelled crabs and crimson-fleshed fresh tuna are among the stars of the 1907 Neo-Gothic fish market hall **(above)**, barely out of reach of the scavenging seagulls.

⑤ Palazzo dei Camerlenghi
This lopsided 1525 palace once imprisoned debtors on the ground floor, while the top floors served as offices for the city *camerlenghi* (treasurers).

6 Gondola Ferry

A must for every visitor is a trip on the *traghetto* ferry across the Grand Canal **(left)** – one of only eight still in operation. Custom dictates that passengers should remain standing.

7 Banco Giro Arcade

Merchants from the East and the West gathered to exchange a variety of goods, including silks and spices, outside the city's first bank set up in 1157, which is now a wine bar.

PLACE NAMES

Rialto market's narrow alleyways carry names such as Orefici (goldsmiths), Pescaria (fishmongers) and Erberia (vegetables), because the same type of shops once stood together. Local eateries for market traders also had evocative names such as Scimia (Monkey) and Do Mori (Two Moors).

8 Ruga degli Orefici

This lovely covered passageway decorated with frescoes has been home to silversmiths, goldsmiths and silk traders since the 1300s.

9 Fabbriche Nuove

Uniformed *carabinieri* (police) patrol the elongated law courts along the Grand Canal. Designed in 1552–5 by Sansovino they are recognizable by their 25 plain arcades.

10 Grand Canal Views

The Erberia, right on the Grand Canal, makes a wonderful spot for boat-watching. Alternatively, wander on to the Rialto Bridge for a different vantage point **(below)**.

NEED TO KNOW

MAP P2 ■ San Polo ■ Fresh produce market: 7:30am–1pm Mon–Sat; Pescheria: 7:30am–1pm Tue–Sat

■ In addition to fresh fruit from the market, picnic supplies can be bought at the delicatessens and bakeries in the neighbourhood.

TOP 10 ★ Torcello

Some of the most breathtaking Byzantine mosaics in the world, found in the lagoon's oldest building, the Torcello basilica, reward those who visit this laid-back island, a beautiful 60-minute ferry ride from northern Venice. From the 5th century, mainlanders fleeing invading Lombards and Huns ventured across tidal flats to found a settlement that grew to 20,000 and lasted 1,000 years. However, few clues to the past remain, as the canals silted up, malaria decimated the population and the power base shifted to Venice once and for all. Today, Torcello is home to a handful of gardeners and fishermen.

Basilica Exterior ①
A miraculous survivor, this striking cathedral was founded in 639, but underwent radical restructuring in 1008. It retains its Romanesque form, light-brick walls and an arcaded 9th-century portico **(right)**.

② Doomsday Mosaics, Basilica
In these 12th–13th-century marvels **(above)**, the Last Judgment is dramatically depicted in superbly restored scenes of devils, angels, wild beasts and fires.

③ Apse Mosaics, Basilica
This moving 13th-century mosaic shows the Virgin in a blue robe with gold fringing, cradling her radiant child. Below are the 12 apostles standing in a meadow of flowers.

④ Iconostasis, Basilica
Marble panels show peacocks drinking at the fountain of eternal life

(left), small lions posing under a tree full of birds, while six columns support 15th-century paintings of the apostles with the Virgin.

⑤ Paving, Basilica
In vivid swirls of colours, rivalling the flooring in Basilica San Marco, are brilliant 11th-century tesserae of stone and glass. Cubes, semicircles and triangles are laid into square designs. The floor level was raised 30 cm (12 inches) during the basilica's reconstruction.

7 Campanile

The views from this simple 55-m (180-ft) bell tower **(left)** reach over the vast expanse of the lagoon, with its meandering canals and tidal flats, to the Adriatic Sea, Venice itself and even north to the Alps on a clear winter's day.

8 Throne of Attila

By popular belief this marble armchair **(below)** was the throne of the king of the Huns, though historical sources claim it was for the island's magistrates.

ATTILA THE HUN

The "Scourge of God", or the King of the Huns, ruled from AD 434 to 453 over an empire that stretched from the Alps and the Baltic towards the Caspian Sea. As part of his campaign against the Roman Empire, Attila attacked Milan, Verona and Padua, and refugees fled to Torcello. Burning the cathedral town of Aquileia gave him great satisfaction – his men raised a hill in Udine so he could enjoy the sight.

9 Museo dell'Estuario

An intriguing, if modest, collection of archaeological finds from the island and priceless treasures from the church are housed in the adjoining Gothic buildings.

NEED TO KNOW

MAP H1 ■ Boat line 12 from the Fondamente Nuove to Burano, then change to boat line 9

Basilica di Santa Maria dell'Assunta: 041 730 119; Open Mar–Oct: 10:30am–5:30pm daily; Nov–Feb: 10am–4:30pm daily; closed 1 Jan, 25 Dec. Adm €5

Campanile: Open Mar–Oct: 10:30am–5:30pm daily; Nov–Feb: 10am–5pm. Adm €5. Audio guide

Santa Fosca: Closed to visitors during services

Museo dell'Estuario: 041 730 761; Open Mar–Oct: 10:30am–5pm Tue–Sun; Nov–Feb: 10am–4:30pm Tue–Sun; closed public hols. Adm €3

6 Santa Fosca

Alongside the basilica is this elegant church based on a Greek cross design, encircled by a five-sided colonnaded portico. The inside of the church is closed to visitors during services.

10 Locanda Cipriani

A favourite of American writer Ernest Hemingway, who stayed here in 1948, this guesthouse **(left)** has a quiet charm that has attracted VIPs since it opened in 1938 (see p148).

TOP 10 ⭐ Campo Santa Margherita

This cheery, picturesque square in the district of Dorsoduro is a hive of activity day in, day out. It owes its name to the Christian martyr St Margaret of Antioch, possibly a fictitious figure, but highly popular in medieval times. Patron saint of expectant mothers, she is depicted in a niche on the square's northern wall with her emblem, the dragon. The square's capacious form, exploited by local children on bicycles and in-line skaters, is due to an ambitious enlargement project in the 1800s which opened up the south end by filling in canals.

1 Ex Chiesa di Santa Margherita

A writhing 14th-century dragon symbolizing the martyrdom of the saint enlivens the foot of the bell tower of the former church. It has been restored by the university as the Auditorium Santa Margherita.

2 Palazzo Foscolo-Corner

This beautiful palace is virtually unchanged since the 1300s and instantly distinguishable by its deep overhanging eaves. A striking Byzantine-style lunette, bearing an inset with the family crest, tops the entrance portal.

3 Scuola Grande dei Carmini

Glorious rooms (below), decorated with Tiepolo's masterpieces, are highlights of this confraternity. The upstairs ceiling shows *St Simon Stock Receiving the Scapular from the Virgin*.

Campo Santa Margherita

4 Calle del Forno

An unusual series of medieval-style projections from a first-floor dwelling, partly held up by brick columns, is one of the most interesting features of this busy thoroughfare leading to Piazzale Roma and the bus terminal. The street is named after a long-gone *forno* (bakery).

5 Scuola dei Varoteri

A splendid bas-relief of the Virgin sheltering a group of trades-men in adoration adorns the former tanners' guild dating from 1725. Because of its isolated position, it was once mistakenly thought to be the house of the city's executioner.

8 Chiesa di Santa Maria dei Carmini

This richly adorned church **(left)** survived Napoleon's suppression of the Carmelite order of monks in the adjoining monastery. Many of its 13th-century features are intact, such as the sculpted entrance porch.

RIO TERRÀ

Rio is a common name for canal, while *terrà* means filled-in. Dating back to the 1300s, the practice of filling in waterways was widespread in the 1800s to provide extra pedestrian space. Some were covered with low-slung arches to keep water flowing, exemplified by Via Garibaldi in Castello *(see p111)*. Later campaigns encouraged the reverse procedure.

9 Corte del Fondaco

A charming covered passageway leads through to this minor courtyard where curious, low, bricked-in arches indicate the former site of a 1700s flour store. The name *fondaco* – or store – is derived from the Arabic word *fonduq*.

10 Rio Nuovo

Excavated in 1932–3 to form a shortcut from Piazzale Roma to the Grand Canal, the canal has been closed to *vaporetti* since the 1990s, due to building damage.

6 The "House of the Moor"

Shakespeare's *Othello* was based on Cristoforo Moro, who was sent to govern Cyprus from 1508. This house at No. 2615 is his former home.

7 Altana Terraces

These timber roof platforms **(right)** were common in Venetian palaces, used by women for bleaching their hair in the sun. They are now used for laundry and partying on summer evenings, and can be seen around Campo Santa Margherita.

NEED TO KNOW

MAP K5

Scuola Grande dei Carmini, Dorsoduro: 041 528 94 20 ■ www. scuolagrandecarmini.it

Open 11am–5pm daily

Adm €5

■ Numerous pizza-slice outlets and bars serving *tramezzini* (sandwiches) and *panini* (rolls) make for a cheap lunch option.

TOP 10 ⭐ Peggy Guggenheim Collection

The delightfully spacious, light-filled Collezione Peggy Guggenheim is home to works by more than 200 contemporary artists representing powerful avant-garde movements such as Cubism, Futurism and Surrealism. The landmark collection, put together by its far-sighted namesake, is housed in the 18th-century Palazzo Venier dei Leoni, known as the "unfinished palace" because of its one-storey construction. As well as the wonderful works of art on display inside the gallery, there is also a striking sculpture garden and the former home of Peggy Guggenheim to visit.

1 The Poet
A wonderful starting point is this portrait (1911) by legendary Spanish artist Pablo Picasso (1881–1973), from his early Cubist period. The figure is executed from a limited palette of ochre and dark browns.

2 Bird in Space
This polished brass sculpture (1932–40) was once classified by US customs as a "stair-rail" and was therefore subject to duty. Its creator was Romanian artist Constantin Brancusi (1876–1957).

3 Attirement of the Bride
This portrayal (1940) of an orange-robed bride assisted by mutant animals and humans (below) is by Max Ernst (1891–1976). The German Surrealist was married to Peggy Guggenheim from 1942 to 1946.

Peggy Guggenheim Collection

Key to Floorplan
- ▩ Gallery
- ▩ Nasher Sculpture Garden

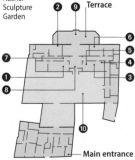

Peggy Guggenheim Collection Floorplan

4 Empire of Light

Magical light effects see darkened trees and a house silhouetted by a street lamp against a contrasting daytime sky with fluffy clouds in this work (1953–4) by René Magritte (1898–1967). The Belgian Surrealist was renowned for his eccentric subjects.

6 Woman Walking

This serene elongated form of a truncated female figure (1932), apparently inspired by Etruscan design, is the recognized trademark of the Swiss artist Alberto Giacometti (1901–66), a short-term participant in the Surrealist movement **(right)**.

7 The Moon Woman

This vibrant canvas (1942) starring a skeletal stick figure with an odd, padded curve is an early work by Jackson Pollock (1912–56), pre-dating his famous "drip" technique.

PEGGY GUGGENHEIM

This heir to a mining fortune (1898–1979) first came to Europe in 1921, quickly fitting into Bohemian Paris. Resolving to "buy a picture a day", she amassed a contemporary art collection before she made Venice her home in 1947. She is fondly remembered by locals here for her faithful dogs and for owning the city's last private gondola.

8 Mobile

This simple masterpiece of movement (1941) by Alexander Calder (1898–1976), which gave its name to all mobiles, hangs in the atrium of Guggenheim's house.

9 Angel of the City

Set on steps leading to the terrace, this bronze horse and rider (1948) by Italian sculptor Marino Marini (1901–80) greet passing boats.

NEED TO KNOW

MAP D5 ■ Fondamenta Venier dei Leoni, Dorsoduro 704 (2nd entrance Calle S Cristoforo, Dorsoduro 701) ■ 041 240 54 11 ■ www.guggenheim-venice.it ■ No flash photography

Open 10am–6pm Wed–Mon; Closed 25 Dec

Adm €15; audio guides

■ Take a break in the coffee shop or on the café's shady verandah for a light snack or a meal.

■ Enjoy the view from the terrace, which looks onto the Grand Canal.

5 Magic Garden

This deliberately child-like piece (1926) by Paul Klee (1879–1940) features blurry shapes and sketched-in faces and buildings.

10 Three Standing Figures

Beautifully placed in the Nasher Sculpture Garden, these sculptures (1953) by Henry Moore (1898–1986) were inspired by Italian bell towers.

The Top 10
of Everything

The world-famous Rialto Bridge, one of
four bridges spanning the Grand Canal

🔟 Moments in History

① AD 421: Birth of Venice

Fleeing the Goths, who were looting their way southwards to Rome, the people of the Veneto sought refuge among the uninhabited islands of their marshy coast. There from the ashes of the Roman past rose the city of Venice. According to tradition on 25 March every year, the Church of San Giacometto is consecrated at Rialto. This is considered the founding date of the city.

The four bronze horses taken from Constantinople

② AD 697: Electing the Doge

Soon after the surrounding coastal area and the lagoon was organized into a duchy, ruled by a "dux" or doge, nominated by the emperor in Constantinople. At the Basilica di San Marco (see pp12–15), the doge was presented to the city following his election. Paoluccio Anafesto was elected first doge.

③ 1204: Siege of Constantinople

Led by the aged and blind doge Enrico Dandolo, the leaders of the Fourth Crusade agreed to attack the capital of Byzantium, as payment for warships supplied by Venice. The treasures taken include four gilded bronze horses. Replicas of the originals appear on the façade of Basilica di San Marco. The city fell in 1204, leaving Venice ruler of Byzantium.

④ 1378–81: Battle of Choggia

The long-standing rivalry between the maritime republics of Venice and Genoa turned into a naval battle in 1378. The attack culminated in 1381 when Venice defeated Genoa at Choggia to win undisputed maritime supremacy in the Adriatic and Mediterranean. The battle led to the Peace of Turin, which heralded the final decline of Genoese hegemony.

Genoese and Venetian naval warships at the Battle of Choggia

1571: Battle of Lepanto
At Lepanto, in Greece, the largest naval battle since antiquity witnessed an alliance of western powers inflict a devastating defeat on the Ottoman fleet.

6 1797: End of the Venetian Republic
After more than a millenium, the first Republic since antiquity fell in 1797 to the invading French troops of Napoleon Bonaparte.

7 1848: First Italian War of Independence
Led by Daniele Manin, the city revolted against Austrian domination, and the rebels proclaimed a new, but short-lived Republic, with the ultimate aim of joining a unified Italy. The city capitulated to the Austrians the following year, after a long siege.

Daniele Manin's statue, Campo Manin

8 1866: Austrian rule ends
The long military and political confrontation between Austria and the Italian states finally resulted in the unification of the Italian territories, including Venice and the Veneto.

9 1966: Floods devastate Venice
In November 1966, the city was hit by the worst floods in its history, sparking concern for the future of the city's delicate and decaying fabric.

10 2008: Grand Canal's fourth bridge opens
The fourth bridge Ponte della Costituzione opened to the public on the night of 11 September, 2008.

A flooded *fondamenta*, Cannaregio

FREQUENTLY ASKED QUESTIONS

1 Is Venice still sinking?
Theoretically, sinking came to a halt when the industries in Marghera stopped pumping out groundwater.

2 What do the buildings stand on?
Pinewood piles overlaid with horizontal planks and marble-like Istrian stone slabs serve as the building foundation.

3 Is swimming in the canal allowed?
Swimming in the canal is forbidden and incurs a hefty fine.

4 How deep is the lagoon?
At its maximum depth, the lagoon is 15 m (49 ft) in the navigable channels dredged for shipping.

5 Is the sea safe for swimming?
Yes, periodic controls for bacterial counts are carried out.

6 Does everyone have a boat?
On average, one in two families possesses a pleasure boat.

7 Can you drink water from the drinking fountains?
Yes, it's the same as tap water and is subject to testing and treatment.

8 How does the house numbering system work?
Within each of the six districts *(sestiere)*, numbers follow the alleyways along one side at a time, taking in branch streets and courtyards when encountered.

9 What are the MOSE floodgates?
This huge dam project aims to protect Venice and its lagoon from exceptionally high flood tides.

10 Why don't people restore the crumbling buildings?
Strict regulations concern façades – only porous stucco can be used as anything else tends to come away and is a hazard for passersby.

TOP 10 Venice Palaces

The striking façade of Ca' Rezzonico

1 Doge's Palace
See pp16–19.

2 Ca' d'Oro
The original lapis lazuli, vermilion and gold façade has long faded, but the breathtaking Gothic delicacy of this "golden palace" (see p103) is intact, with exquisite marble tracery and arcaded loggias crafted by 15th-century stonemasons.

Gothic architecture of Ca' d'Oro

3 Ca' Foscari
MAP L5 ■ Calle Foscari, Dorsoduro 3246 ■ Open for pre-booked guided tours only ■ www.unive.it

Set on a strategic bend of the Grand Canal, this excellent example of late Gothic architecture has a series of mullioned windows facing the water, surmounted by an Istrian stone frieze. Once home to the long-ruling Doge Francesco Foscari, today it is part of the University of Venice.

4 Ca' Rezzonico
MAP L5 ■ Fondamenta Rezzonico, Dorsoduro 3136 ■ Open 10am–5pm Wed–Mon ■ Adm ■ www.visitmuve.it

This glittering palace adorned with Tiepolo ceiling frescoes, majestic Murano glass chandeliers and elaborate carved period furniture is now home to the Museum of 18th-century Venetian Life.

5 Palazzo Vendramin-Calergi
This stately Renaissance residence (see p67) built by architects Lombardo and Coducci in the late 15th century was home to a string of noble families including the Cretan merchant Calergi in 1589. Another famed tenant was composer Richard Wagner, who spent his final years here. The palace is now home to the glittering City Casino.

6 Ca' Dario
Framed multicoloured round stones (tondi) embellish this privately owned, asymmetrical palace (see p25) dating from 1486. It was built for Giovanni Dario, ambassador to Constantinople, where he negotiated a peace treaty bringing long-term hostilities between Venice and the Turks to a temporary halt.

7 Palazzo Mastelli

MAP D1 ■ Rio della Madonna dell'Orto, Cannaregio 3932 ■ Closed to public

This eclectic delight, on a peaceful back canal of Cannaregio, was the abode of three merchant brothers from Morea on the Peloponnese from 1112. Their turbaned likenesses in stone adorn neighbouring Campo dei Mori (see p104). Lions, birds and a prominent camel can be picked out on the Gothic façade.

8 Palazzi Contarini degli Scrigni e Corfu

MAP B5 ■ Calle Contarini Corfu, Dorsoduro 1057 ■ Closed to public

A 15th-century residence, enlarged by architect Vincenzo Scamozzi for the 17th-century proprietor Contarini "of the coffers" (scrigni), so-called for the vast wealth of his family. The roof-top "folly" acted as a useful observatory for astronomers.

9 Palazzo Barbaro

MAP M6 ■ Rio dell'Orso, S Marco 2840 ■ Closed to public

Cole Porter, Diaghilev, Monet and Whistler are just a few former guests of this private double palace, courtesy of the 19th-century Curtis family from Boston. Henry James (see p53) wrote The Aspern Papers here and used it as the setting for The Wings of a Dove.

10 Palazzo Pisani-Moretta

MAP M4 ■ Ramo Pisani e Barbarigo, S Polo 2766 ■ Open for private functions only

Venue of a fabulous masked ball during Carnival, when VIP guests glide in gondolas to the candlelit Gothic façade on the Grand Canal. Tiepolo and Guarana contributed to the interior Baroque decorations.

Palazzo Pisani-Moretta

TOP 10 ARCHITECTURAL FEATURES OF A PALAZZO

Typical canal entrance

1 Canal Entrance
This is where the family's private gondolas were moored and visitors were received.

2 Piano Nobile
The high-ceilinged first floor of a palazzo hosts the sumptuous salons and family's living quarters.

3 Façade
Usually fronting a canal, this was the only exterior wall decorated with a costly stone overlay to impress visitors.

4 Funnel-Shaped Chimneys
These and many other variations punctuate rooftops, their long shafts often running along outside walls.

5 Kitchen
This was always located on the ground floor for practical reasons.

6 Central Well
This received filtered rain water for the palazzo's main water supply.

7 Entrance Portal
The importance of the main entrance was usually indicated by the distinctive family crest.

8 Enclosed Courtyard
This bustling area, usually with store rooms, was often used for the family's business transactions.

9 Altana Roof Terrace-Platform
These open-air areas were traditionally used for hanging out the washing or bleaching hair in the sun.

10 Land Access
Private gondolas rendered this relatively unimportant and hence, a narrow alley sufficed in its stead.

Venice Churches

1 ### Basilica di San Marco
See pp12–15.

2 ### Santa Maria Gloriosa dei Frari
See pp32–3.

Santi Giovanni e Paolo

3 ### Santi Giovanni e Paolo
MAP E3 ■ Campo SS Giovanni e Paolo, Castello ■ Open 9am–6pm Mon–Sat, noon–6pm Sun ■ Adm ■ www.basilicasantigiovanniepaolo.it

The monumental tombs of 25 doges take pride of place in this Gothic giant, built by Dominican friars from the 13th to 15th centuries. Among them is the tribute to Pietro Mocenigo for his valorous struggle to defend Venice's eastern colonies against the Turks (west wall). Inside are numerous works of art including splendid paintings by Veronese and a polyptych (1465) by Giovanni Bellini.

4 ### Santa Maria dei Miracoli
A favourite among Venetians for weddings, Pietro Lombardo's showcase (1481–9) is resplendent again after restoration to deal with rising damp. The problem is not new – in Renaissance times marble slabs were affixed to the brick exterior with a cavity left for air flow. The ceiling gleams with gilt miniatures of holy figures *(see p104)*.

5 ### San Zaccaria
MAP F4 ■ Campo S Zaccaria, Castello ■ Open 10am–noon, 4–6pm Mon–Sat, 4–6pm Sun & public hols ■ Adm (chapels & crypt)

An intricately decorated 15th-century façade by Coducci and, inside, Giovanni Bellini's superb *Madonna and Saints* (1505) are highlights of this 9th-century church. The adjoining convent, now a police station, used to host puppet shows to entertain the nuns.

6 ### San Giorgio Maggiore
MAP F5 ■ Isola di S Giorgio Maggiore ■ Open daily (times can vary) ■ Adm (bell tower)

Palladio's harmoniously proportioned church (1566–1610), inspired by Greek temple design, stands across the water from Piazza San Marco. The interior is offset by two dynamic paintings by Tintoretto from 1594, *The Last Supper* and *Gathering the Manna*, on the chancel walls. The bell tower offers views over Venice. Don't miss the monks' Gregorian chants every Sunday at 11am.

7 ### Santa Maria della Salute
MAP D5 ■ Campo della Salute, Dorsoduro ■ Open 9:30am–noon, 3–5:30pm daily ■ Adm (sacristy)

A remarkable Baroque church dominating the southernmost entrance to the Grand Canal, Santa Maria della Salute's silhouette has become one of Venice's most well-known landmarks. Designed by architect Longhena in 1630, it has a spacious, light-filled interior, while the altar houses a precious Byzantine icon. Dramatic works by Titian and Tintoretto can be appreciated in the sacristy.

8 Chiesa di San Sebastiano

Renaissance painter Paolo Veronese (1528–88) spent a large proportion of his life joyously decorating the ceiling, walls, organ doors and altar of this unassuming 16th-century church *(see p98)*, and was buried among his colourful masterpieces.

9 Madonna dell'Orto

MAP D1 ■ Campo Madonna dell'Orto, Cannaregio ■ Open 10am–5pm Mon–Sat, noon–5pm Sun ■ Adm ■ www.madonnadellorto.org

Eleven huge canvases by devout parishioner Tintoretto enhance this graceful Gothic church. Two master-pieces flank the high altar – the gruesome *The Last Judgment* and the soaring grandeur of *The Making of the Golden Calf*, both thought to have been painted about 1563.

Madonna dell'Orto

10 San Pantalon

MAP K4 ■ Campo S Pantalon, Dorsoduro ■ Open 10am–noon, 1–3pm Mon–Sat ■ www.sanpantalon.it

Two treasures lurk behind a ramshackle façade: a nail from the True Cross in a rich Gothic altar and the overwhelming ceiling (1680–1704) by Gian Antonio Fumiani, a labour of love that ended when he purportedly plunged from the scaffolding to his death.

TOP 10 SHRINES AND TABERNACLES

Flowers at a shrine to St Anthony

1 St Anthony
MAP D2 ■ Calle Larga, Cannaregio
This 1668 "wardrobe" is full of fresh flower offerings.

2 Sottoportego de la Madonna
MAP D3 ■ Sant' Aponal, S Polo
Pope Alexander III took refuge here from Emperor Barbarossa in 1177.

3 Gondolier's Shrine
MAP R5 ■ Ponte della Paglia, S Marco
A 1583 Madonna greets boats approaching the bridge.

4 Corte Nova
MAP G4 ■ Castello
Painted images over a lace-trimmed mantlepiece.

5 Covered Passageway
MAP F4 ■ Calle Zorzi, Castello
The Virgin's protection has been implored here against plague and enemy attacks.

6 Scuola Grande della Misericordia
MAP D2 ■ Cannaregio
Carvings of laden boats seek protection for the ferries, which set out from here.

7 Corte de Ca' Sarasina
MAP H5 ■ Castello
Shrine dating back to the 1600s in memory of the dead.

8 Ponte del Fontego
MAP F3 ■ Campo S Giustina, Castello
A Neo-Classical bridge featuring gondola bas-reliefs.

9 Gondola Traghetto Point
MAP L4 ■ S Tomà, S Polo
Madonna on a pole in the Grand Canal.

10 Boatmen's Pole
Tabernacle midway on the San Giuliano–Venice channel.

Outstanding Venetians

1 Marco Polo

Legendary Cathay and the kingdom of the mighty Kublai Khan took pride of place in the great explorer Marco Polo's best-selling account of his 20-year odyssey to the Far East, *Book of the Marvels of the World*. Son of a Venetian merchant, Polo (1254–1324) is responsible for the introduction of pasta and window blinds to the western world.

Marco Polo

2 Antonio Vivaldi

Vivaldi (1678–1741) was both an accomplished musician and an influential Baroque composer. Of his 500 concertos, *The Four Seasons* is the best known. J S Bach was a noted fan and transcribed ten of the Italian's concertos. Vivaldi spent extended periods teaching music at the Pietà home for girls *(see p109)*.

3 Giacomo Casanova

This marvellous romantic figure (1725–98) was variously a diplomat, scholar, trainee priest, adventurer, gambler, notary's clerk, violinist, womanizer, exile, millionaire, writer and spy. Casanova was imprisoned in the Doge's Palace *(see pp16–19)* on charges of being a magician, from where he effected an infamously daring escape.

Giacomo Casanova

4 Claudio Monteverdi

This late Renaissance madrigalist (1567–1643) is attributed with the introduction of the solo voice to theatre. His opera *Proserpina Rapita* was the first to be performed in Venice. After long periods at the court of the Gonzagas, he accepted an appointment at the Basilica di San Marco and worked for the Scuola Grande di San Rocco *(see p89)*.

5 John Cabot

Italian navigator Giovanni Caboto, or John Cabot (1450–99), and his sons were authorized by Henry VII of England to search for new lands with the aim of furthering trade. Believing himself on the northeast coast of Asia, he discovered Newfoundland in Canada and claimed it for England, opening up cod fishing.

6 Elena Lucrezia Corner Piscopia

It was inconceivable for the church in 1678 that a woman should teach religion, so the University of Padua awarded this child prodigy and the first woman graduate (1646–84) a degree in philosophy, instead of one in theology to which she aspired.

7 Daniele Manin

Organizer of the 1848 rebellion against Austrian rule, the Venetian patriot (1804–57) is commemorated by a statue in Campo Manin. An independent "republic" was declared and survived 17 months of bombardments and even cholera, concluding with Manin's exile to Paris.

8 Paolo Sarpi

When the pope excommunicated Venice for insubordination, involving restrictions on church construction and the refusal to hand over two priests on criminal charges, Sarpi (1552–1623) resolved the rupture. A patriot and theologian, he was an advocate of division between State and Church.

Caterina Cornaro

9 Caterina Cornaro

This Venetian noblewoman (1454–1510) married the king of Cyprus then allegedly poisoned him, thus securing the strategic island for Venice. Her return to the city was an occasion of great pomp, recalled to this day in a waterborne procession during the Regata Storica (see p76). Cornaro's reward was the hilltown of Asolo.

10 Luigi Nono

This musician (1924–90) made milestone progress in the field of electronic music, and an archive named after him was set up in Venice in 1993. A committed Communist, his works were often provocative.

Avant-garde composer Luigi Nono

🔟 Writers and Venice

Teatro Comunale Carlo Goldoni

1 Carlo Goldoni
"Italy's Molière" (1707–93) is celebrated at the Venetian theatre named in his honour (see p65). Performances of his lively, witty comedies are staged in Venetian dialect and peopled with recognizable local characters. The prolific playwright moved to Paris and was rewarded with a royal pension, but he died destitute due to the French Revolution.

2 Thomas Mann
The sombre 1912 novel *Death in Venice* was both written and set in Venice and the Lido resort by the German Nobel Prize-winner (1875–1955). It tells the story of an ageing writer in dire need of relaxation who visits the city, but in the wake of an impossible infatuation slowly succumbs to the spreading cholera epidemic and dies.

3 William Shakespeare
Although he never visited Italy, let alone Venice, the English Bard (1564–1616) used accounts by contemporary travellers for the plots of *The Merchant of Venice* and *Othello*, portraying a city buzzing with trade and intrigue. *Romeo and Juliet* is set in nearby Verona (see p130).

William Shakespeare

4 Thomas Coryate
The very first English-language traveller to write a detailed description of Venice, this eccentric gentleman from Somerset, England (1577–1617) compiled *Crudities, with Observations of Venice* (1611): "Such is the rarenesse of the situation of Venice, that it doth even amaze and drive into admiration all strangers that upon their first arrival behold the same."

5 Johann Wolfgang von Goethe
The story goes that this German literary giant (1749–1832) had his first ever view of the sea from Venice's Campanile.

His first visit to the city and Italy was an experience of personal renewal. The account, published as *Italian Journey* (1786–8), is considered an early classic of travel literature.

Johann Wolfgang von Goethe

6 Lord Byron
Eccentricities such as a menagerie of foxes and monkeys, not to mention swimming feats in the Grand Canal, made the English Romantic poet (1788–1824) something of a legend during his three-year sojourn here. His Venice-inspired work included *The Two Foscari* and the fourth canto of his autobiographical work *Childe Harold's Pilgrimage*.

7 John Ruskin
The meticulous, if opinionated, labour of love of this British art critic (1819–1900), *The Stones of Venice*, was the first work to focus the attention of visitors on the city's unique architectural heritage

and Gothic style, as opposed to the art. The book was largely the outcome of an 1849 visit to the city.

8 Henry James

The leitmotif of this US novelist (1843–1916) was the contrast between what he saw as the spontaneity of the New World and the staidness of Europe. Between 1872 and 1909 he compiled *Italian Hours*, a "travel diary", with plenty of comments on Venice.

Ernest Hemingway

9 Ernest Hemingway

This US Nobel Prize-winner (1899–1961) experienced Italy as a volunteer ambulance driver in World War I (recounted in *A Farewell to Arms*) and was wounded near Treviso. *Across the River and into the Trees* is set in Harry's Bar *(see p25)*.

10 Charles Dickens

The great English novelist (1812–70) spent a brief period in Venice during a tour of Italy, and the city inspired a dream sequence in his work *Pictures from Italy* (1846).

Illustration from "An Italian Dream" in Dickens's *Pictures from Italy*

TOP 10 BACKGROUND READS

***Death in Venice* film adaptation**

1 Death in Venice, Thomas Mann
A portrayal of desire and decadence amid the fog.

2 Venice, Jan Morris
An expert account of the delights of the city and its maritime history.

3 Venice, an Anthology Guide, Milton Grundy
A guide around town, seen through the eyes of famous writers.

4 Ruskin's Venice, editor Arnold Whittick
A very readable version of Ruskin's landmark work.

5 Stone Virgin, Barry Unsworth
A mystery involving the 15th-century statue of a famous courtesan.

6 Casanova, or the Art of Happiness, Lydia Flem
An inspired biography of the famous seducer *(see p50)*.

7 Dead Lagoon, Michael Dibdin
Detective Aurelio Zen navigates Venice's murky waters fraught with unease and intrigue.

8 The Architecture of Venice, Deborah Howard
An unbeatable architectural classic.

9 Venice: A Maritime Republic, Frederic C. Lane
A comprehensive history of the city's maritime prowess.

10 Acqua Alta, Donna Leon
From the best-selling mystery series featuring detective Guido Brunetti.

Artists in Venice

The Madonna of the Meadow (1505) by Giovanni Bellini

1 Giovanni Bellini

Giovanni Bellini (1430–1516), with his father Jacopo and brother Gentile, made Venice one of the greatest centres of Renaissance art. His anatomy studies added great precision to his work. His trademarks are radiant Madonnas, serene St Peters and brilliant satiny robes.

2 Canaletto (Giovanni Antonio Canal)

Famous for his landscapes of Venice and England, Canaletto (1697–1768) thrived under the patronage of the British consul Joseph Smith. Unfortunately, very few of his paintings can be seen in Venice.

3 Titian (Tiziano Vecellio)

A native of the Cadore region, whose awe-inspiring Dolomite peaks often feature in his highly coloured dynamic compositions, Titian (1488–1576) came to Venice when young and studied under Giovanni Bellini.

4 Jacopo Tintoretto

The great Mannerist of the late Renaissance, Tintoretto (1518–94) produced huge, glowing canvases, seen at his main showcase the Scuola Grande di San Rocco *(see p89)*, as well as his parish church Madonna dell'Orto *(see p49)*.

5 Paolo Veronese

Foremost painter of the Venetian School, Veronese (1528–88) created huge canvases in classical settings and teeming with people. They are on display in the Doge's Palace *(see pp16–19)* and the Chiesa di San Sebastiano *(see p98)*.

6 Giambattista Tiepolo

Tiepolo (1696–1770) is admired for his luminous poetic frescoes from the Rococo period, such as those he was commissioned to paint

View of the Grand Canal (late 1720s) by Canaletto

on the ceiling of the Scuola Grande dei Carmini in Dorsoduro *(see p38)*. The villas near Vicenza also feature his work; however, his best work is in the Residenz, Würzburg.

7 Vittorio Carpaccio

This Renaissance master (1465–1525) delighted in remarkably detailed scenes of daily life in contemporary Venice. His original narrative style and marvellous command of light characterize his many cycles on display at the Accademia galleries *(see p31)* and the Scuola di San Giorgio degli Schiavoni *(see p57)*.

8 Giorgione

A native of Castelfranco Veneto, Giorgione (1477–1510) came to Venice when young to serve as an apprentice under Giovanni Bellini. In his brief life, he produced memorable mood works that he never signed. One of his most famous works, *The Tempest*, can be seen in the Accademia *(see p30)*.

Virgin and Child (1504) by Giorgione

9 Pietro Longhi

Longhi (1702–85) painted witty scenes of the everyday life of the well-to-do folk in Venice. Examples of his work can be admired at the Fondazione Querini Stampalia *(see p56)*, as well as in Ca' Rezzonico *(see p46)*. Many figures are wearing the traditional Venetian mask.

10 Francesco Guardi

A prolific landscape painter, Guardi (1712–93) successfully captured the light and atmosphere of Venice in decline. People are depicted as insignificant and powerless against landscapes that incorporate the lagoon and islands. His canvases are on display at Ca' Rezzonico *(see p46)*.

TOP 10 VENICE ARCHITECTS

Chiesa del Santissimo Redentore, by Andrea Palladio

1 Andrea Palladio *(1508–80)*
Regarded as one of the most influential architects of the western world, Palladio designed Classical villas in the Veneto and churches in Venice.

2 Jacopo Sansovino *(1486–1570)*
Outstanding architect who trained under – and took his name from – sculptor Andrea Sansovino. Examples of Jacopo's work are the Libreria *(see p22)* and Zecca.

3 Baldassare Longhena *(1598–1682)*
Longhena's masterpiece, Santa Maria della Salute, was designed when he was just 26, but his flamboyant style is also seen in Ca' Rezzonico *(see p46)*.

4 Pietro Lombardo *(1435–1515)*
Lombardy native Pietro was director of works at the Doge's Palace. His trademark leafy bas-relief pattern is also seen at Santa Maria dei Miracoli *(see p104)*.

5 Mauro Coducci *(c.1440–1504)*
The Renaissance designs of Lombardy native Coducci can be seen in Palazzo Vendramin-Calergi *(see p67)*.

6 Bartolomeo Bon *(1374–1464)*
Sculptor/architect Bon's designs were the basis for the church and Scuola di San Rocco and the Ca' d'Oro *(see p46)*.

7 Michele Sanmicheli *(1484–1559)*
Original military fortification designs by this Mannerist architect are found in his home town of Verona.

8 Antonio Da Ponte *(1512–95)*
This engineer and architect is well known for the Rialto Bridge *(see p58)*.

9 Giannantonio Selva *(1757–1819)*
In Venice, Selva is best known for the elegant Fenice theatre *(see p64)*.

10 Carlo Scarpa *(1906–78)*
Modernist Scarpa reorganized both the Accademia and the Querini Stampalia along Japanese-inspired lines.

🔟 Museums and Galleries

1 Accademia Galleries
See pp30–31.

2 Museo del Merletto
MAP H1 ■ Piazza Baldassare Galuppi 187, Burano ■ Open Apr–Oct: 10am–6pm Tue–Sun (to 5pm Nov–Mar) ■ Adm ■ museomerletto. visitmuve.it

A must for craft-lovers is the lacemaking island of Burano and this precious display of more than 200 rare lace items, documenting a 500-year history.

3 Museo del Vetro
MAP G2 ■ Fondamenta Giustiniani 8, Murano ■ Open Apr–Oct: 10am–6pm daily (to 5pm Nov–Mar) ■ Adm ■ www. visitmuve.it

A phenomenal chandelier from 1864, constructed from 356 handmade pieces, weighing 330 kg (730 lb) and measuring nearly 7 m (23 ft) in circumference and 4-m (13-ft) high, is the star of this glass museum in the Palazzo Giustiniani. Other exhibits include Phoenician phials, blown vases, ruby chalices, exquisite mirrors and the

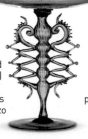

Murano glassware at Museo del Vetro

famed kaleidoscopic beads that were once traded worldwide.

4 Palazzo Grassi
This landmark collection (see p82) of contemporary art, housed in a palace on the Grand Canal, is renewed on a regular basis. The inspirational sister gallery is Punta della Dogana (see p98).

5 Fondazione Querini Stampalia
MAP R4 ■ Campo S Maria Formosa, Castello 5252 ■ Open 10am–6pm Tue–Sun ■ www.querini stampalia.org

This unmissable Renaissance palace was the bequest of Giovanni Querini in 1868, the last member of the illustrious dynasty, on the condition that the library be made available "particularly in the evenings for the convenience of scholars". The immaculately restored palace-museum houses fascinating scenes of public and private life by Gabriel Bella and Pietro Longhi, as well as Carlo Scarpa's Modernist creations.

6 Museo Correr

A tremendous number of priceless artworks and a miscellany of items on Venice's history are housed in this fine museum on Piazza San Marco (see p22).

Museo Correr

7 Ca' Pesaro Galleria d'Arte Moderna

MAP N1 ▪ Fondamenta Ca' Pesaro, S Croce 2076 ▪ Open Apr–Oct: 10am–6pm Tue–Sun (to 5pm Nov–Mar) ▪ Adm ▪ www.visitmuve.it

A Baroque triumph of a palace, Ca' Pesaro's interior, in contrast, houses works by European 19th- and 20th-century masters such as Marc Chagall and Gustave Klimt, including a strong collection of Italian works.

November 1870 by Telemaco Signorini in the Ca' Pesaro Galleria

8 Scuola di San Giorgio degli Schiavoni

MAP F4 ▪ Calle dei Furlani, Castello 3259 ▪ Open 1:30–5:30pm Mon, 9:30am–5:30pm Tue–Sat, 9:30am–1:30pm Sun & pub hols ▪ Adm

The finest works by Vittorio Carpaccio can be seen at the confraternity of the Slavs (Schiavoni). *Slaying The Dragon* is one of the scenes from the lives of Dalmatian saints, which were painted between 1502 and 1507.

9 Scuola Grande di San Rocco

The San Rocco (see p89) confraternity has been turned into a gallery to display its spectacular collection of works by Tintoretto. The artist won the commission hands down – not content with a sketch, he completed an entire canvas. He then spent 23 years devoting himself to the cycle of 60 inspired Old and New Testament scenes, culminating in the breath-taking *Crucifixion* (1565). These masterpieces are the crowning glory of Tintoretto's life work.

Doge's ceremonial barge at the Museo Storico Navale

10 Museo Storico Navale

MAP G4 ▪ Campo S Biagio, Castello 2148 ▪ Open 10am–6pm daily (last adm 5pm) ▪ Adm ▪ www.visitmuve.it

Watercraft galore are found here, and almost an entire floor is dedicated to the golden age of the Venetian Republic's naval past. However, the highlight is the replica of the Doge's ceremonial barge, *Bucintoro*, decorated with allegorical statues.

Bridges

1 Bridge of Sighs
MAP R5

This evocatively named bridge *(see p17)* (known as Ponte dei Sospiri in Italian) once led convicts from the beautiful Doge's Palace to the horrors of the adjacent prisons.

2 Rialto Bridge
MAP P3

The design of this most famous Venetian bridge *(see p34)* at the narrowest point of the Grand Canal was hotly contested – leading 16th-century architects Michelangelo, Sansovino and Palladio entered the competition, but lost out to Antonio da Ponte. There were two previous bridges on this site; a flimsy timber bridge that collapsed in 1444 under the weight of a crowd, then a drawbridge, which would be raised for the passage of tall-masted sailing ships.

3 Ponte dei Tre Archi
MAP B1

A favourite subject for artists, this unusual three-arched high bridge dating from 1688 crosses the Cannaregio canal close to where it joins the lagoon. It was the work of engineer Andrea Tirali, nicknamed Tiranno (the tyrant) by his employees.

Ponte dei Tre Archi

4 Ponte degli Scalzi
MAP J1

One of the city's most marvellous lookout points, over fascinating palaces and boats, can be found at the highest point of this elegant 40-m- (130-ft-) long bridge, which rises 7 m (23 ft) above the Grand Canal. Named after the nearby monastery of bare-footed monks, this 1934 structure in Istrian stone by Eugenio Miozzi replaced an Austrian-built iron bridge.

Ponte della Libertà

5 Ponte della Libertà
MAP A1

Truth and irony combine in the name of this 3.6-km (2-mile) "Bridge of Freedom": the first full link between the mainland and Venice was put in place in 1933, when Italy was living under Fascism. The construction was preceded 86 years earlier by the Austrian-built railway bridge across the lagoon. Before that, the city relied entirely on boats.

6 Ponte dei Pugni
MAP K5

Pugni (fistfights) between rival clans took place here until 1705 when they were outlawed for their violence. Stone footprints marked the starting point of the combat, but contestants usually ended up in the canal.

7 Bridge with No Parapet
MAP D2

One of only two remaining bridges with no side protection, this one spans a quiet side canal in Cannaregio. The other is the Ponte del Diavolo on Torcello.

8 Ponte delle Tette
MAP M2

When an increase in the practice of sodomy was recorded in the 1400s, the city's prostitutes were encouraged to display their feminine wares at the windows over the "Bridge of Breasts".

9 Tre Ponti
MAP B3

Not three but five interlocking bridges span the Rio Novo canal near Piazzale Roma. The timber and stone structures afford views taking in 13 other bridges.

Tre Ponti three-way bridge

10 Ponte della Costituzione
MAP B3

Also known as the Ponte di Calatrava, after its designer Santiago Calatrava, this fourth Grand Canal is modelled on a gondola's hull. It has attracted criticism since its 2008 inauguration due its minimalist modern design and the high cost of construction.

Bridge with No Parapet, over Rio di San Felice

🔟 Off the Beaten Track

1 Cloister of Sant'Apollonia

MAP R4 ■ Ponte della Canonica, Castello 4312 ■ Open 10am–7pm daily

Literally steps away from Piazza San Marco, Venice's only original Romanesque cloister boasts a lovely courtyard with twin-columned arcades. A quiet spot, it is part of the Museo Diocesano d'Arte Sacra.

Sant'Elena

Cloister of Sant'Apollonia

2 Rio Terrà Rampani

MAP M2 ■ San Polo

Just around the corner from Ponte delle Tette (Bridge of Breasts; see p59) is this quiet thoroughfare. Referred to as the "Carampane" (Ca' Rampani), it has been Venice's red-light district since 1421. The city had some 11,600 officially registered courtesans in the 1500s.

3 Sant'Elena

MAP H6

Located in the far eastern extremity of Venice, this quiet residential islet has marvellous shady parkland on the waterfront. Children can enjoy the skating rink and playground while parents relax at laidback cafés.

4 Celestia to Bacini Walkway

MAP G3 ■ Castello

This unusual walkway clings to a perimeter wall of the ancient Arsenale shipyard in a rather neglected zone of Castello. It makes for an atmospheric walk, offering marvellous views over the lagoon and leading to a cluster of old workers' dwellings.

5 Corte dell'Anatomia

MAP L2 ■ S Croce

This peaceful courtyard was named after the anatomy theatre that existed here in 1368. Much later, in 1671, in neighbouring Campo San Giacomo dell'Orio, a College of Anatomy was established in what is now a separate building with an attractive trellis draped with vines.

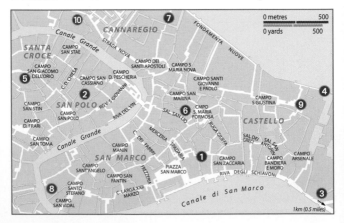

Calle del Paradiso

(Jesuit) church, it is flanked by the cavernous Crociferi complex, erstwhile monastery, then barracks, now student lodgings. Wander inside to admire the cloisters and the canal-side café.

8 Corte del Duca Sforza
MAP L6 ▪ San Marco

This picturesque courtyard, which opens on to the Grand Canal, is surprisingly well hidden. It takes its name from the Duke of Milan who took over a partially constructed palace here in 1461, though work went no further than the diamond-point ashlar on the façade. The artist Titian used the building as a studio while he was working on the Doge's Palace *(see pp16–19)*.

9 Campo della Celestia
MAP G3 ▪ Castello

Now a tranquil residential spot, back in the 1200s this square saw plenty of comings and goings due to the riotous behaviour of the sisters in the Cistercian convent. The first archive of city affairs was established here under Napoleon.

10 Campo della Maddalena
MAP D2 ▪ Cannaregio

Just off the main thoroughfare Strada Nova, you will find this lovely raised square. It is often used as a film location, due to the fact that it remains all but unchanged since medieval times. Its modest houses are topped with a fascinating range of chimneys.

6 Calle del Paradiso
MAP R3 ▪ Castello, San Lio

This attractive alley just off the busy San Lio thoroughfare is lined with medieval-style overhangs, as well as restaurants and shops. The name comes from the delightful lopsided, sculptured 15th-century arch depicting the Virgin and her devotees at the end.

7 Campo dei Gesuiti
MAP E2 ▪ Cannaregio

A favourite spot for children to play in, this is a spacious neighbourhood square. In addition to the Gesuiti

Unspoilt and appealing Campo della Maddalena

⓾ Places for Children

The Giardini in Castello, a great place for children to let off steam

① Play Areas

Children tired of art and architecture can release their energy at well-equipped playgrounds with slides, swings and frames at Parco Savorgnan near Ponte delle Guglie in Cannaregio and the fenced-in waterfront park at Giardini in Castello *(see p111)*. The vast shady green expanse of Sant'Elena even boasts a modest skating rink and an artificial climbing wall. Otherwise, make friends with the city kids as they kick footballs or cycle around Campo San Polo on an afternoon.

② Ferry Trips

Restful for adults, exciting for youngsters, the varied boat lines are an ideal way for families to appreciate the joys of the city. Get older children to plan trips on the route maps, but avoid the outside seating on the *vaporetto* with toddlers. For an extended trip, take the majestic double-decker *motonave* over to Lido and Punta Sabbioni *(see p119)*.

③ Glassmaking Demonstrations

Magic moments are guaranteed as children are transfixed by skilful craftsmen blowing blobs of molten glass into fine vases, or moulding coloured rods into myriad animal shapes. Small workshops are dotted all over Venice, while Murano *(see p117)* has more large-scale furnaces – demonstrations are free, on the condition that you stroll through the showroom afterwards.

④ Museo di Storia Naturale

MAP L1 ▪ Salizzada del Fondaco dei Turchi, S Croce 1730 ▪ 041 275 02 06 ▪ Open Jun–Oct: 10am–6pm Tue–Sun; Nov–May: 9am–5pm Tue–Fri, 10am–6pm Sat & Sun ▪ Adm (last admission 1 hour before closing) ▪ www.visitmuve.it

The star of the natural history museum is a 3.6-m- (12-ft-) tall, 7-m- (23-ft-) long skeleton of the dinosaur *Ouranosaurus nigeriensis*, found in the Sahara Desert by Giancarlo Ligabue. Don't miss the aquarium.

Museo di Storia Naturale

Boat in the Museo Storico Navale

5 Museo Storico Navale

Easily the best city museum (see p57) for children, this three-floor haven of shipbuilding includes Chinese junks and exhibits from World War II, such as the famed torpedoes guided by Italian Navy divers, responsible for sinking British warships.

6 Peggy Guggenheim Collection

Every Sunday the museum (see pp40–41) hosts Art4Family, free educational workshops in English and Italian, run by artists and students from the Venice Academy of Fine Arts, for children aged 4 to 10 and their parents. You must book in advance.

7 Lanterna Magica

MAP K5 ■ Campo San Barnaba, Dorsoduro 2808

Standing on a picture-postcard bridge, this delightful toy emporium caters for kids both young and old. Owners Marco and Francesco are veteran game designers specializing in Tolkien-related board games, making this a prime destination for gamer geeks.

8 Doge's Palace Prisons and Armoury

Children are thrilled by the spooky labyrinth of narrow passageways through the palace's (see pp16–19) erstwhile prisons, and it's fun deciphering the graffiti scratched on the walls by inmates over the centuries. In the armoury,

hunt out the unusual child-sized suit from the 16th century, along with the protection for horses.

9 Mistero e Magia

MAP R4 ■ Ruga Giuffa, Castello 4925

Run by a real magician, this shop is full of essentials such as wands, hats, and books revealing the tricks of the trade in Italian and English.

10 Visiting the Lido

If younger children are starting to tire of the galleries and museums, take them to play at the Lido (see pp122–5). The free beaches offer hours of fun and not just in the summer. Bikes can also be hired.

Beach at the Lido

🔟 Entertainment Venues

Stunning interior of Teatro La Fenice

① Teatro La Fenice

MAP N5 ■ Tickets from Venezia Unica offices at the theatre (041 2424) or online ■ www.teatrolafenice.it

World-famous opera and concert performances are held at this glorious theatre *(see p81)*, re-inaugurated in December 2003. Productions range from Verdi and Rossini to contemporary composers.

② Teatro Malibran

MAP Q2 ■ Corte del Teatro Malibran, Cannaregio ■ Tickets from Venezia Unica offices at the theatre (041 2424)

In a quiet square near Rialto stands the Malibran Theatre, re-inaugurated in 2001 to take on part of the Fenice's productions. Dating back to 1678 as Teatro Grimani, it was renamed after the 19th-century Spanish mezzo-soprano Maria Malibran.

Teatro Malibran

③ Films in English

MAP M1 ■ Videoteca Pasinetti: Salizzada San Stae, Santa Croce 1991 ■ 041 274 71 40 ■ www.comune. venezia.it ■ Venice Film Festival: 041 521 87 11 ■ www.labiennale.org

The Venice Film Library occasionally shows films in English during the winter. In late summer the local cinemas screen some of the highlights from the Venice Film Festival.

④ Palazzo Barbarigo Minotto

MAP D5 ■ Fondamenta Duodo o Barbarigo, San Marco 2504 ■ 340 971 72 72 ■ www.musicapalazzo.com

A great way to experience grand operas, Musica a Palazzo performs each act of an opera in a different hall of the grand Palazzo Barbarigo Minotto. The travelling opera is a revival of a tradition that began at the end of the 19th century.

⑤ Vivaldi Concerts

MAP Q4 ■ Ateneo San Basso, Piazzetta dei Leoncini, San Marco ■ 041 528 28 25 ■ www.virtuosidi venezia.com

Inspiring, atmospheric performances of Vivaldi's music can be enjoyed in the intimate setting of Ateneo San Basso, which is just off Piazza San Marco. Tickets are available at agencies, hotels or directly from the palace.

⑥ Chamber Music

MAP M6 ■ Campo S Vidal, S Marco 2862 ■ 041 277 05 61 ■ www.interpretiveneziani.com

While listening to the uplifting notes of Vivaldi's *Four Seasons* or a masterpiece from Bach or Benedetto Marcello, this is the perfect spot to take a moment to unwind and relax from the day's hectic sightseeing. The Church of San Vidal was rebuilt around 1700 and has a spacious interior.

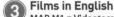

Concerts in Costume
MAP J5 ■ Scuola Grande dei Carmini, Campo S Margherita, Dorsoduro ■ 041 528 ■ www.musicainmaschera.it

Talented young singers and musicians perform comic operas at the Scuola Grande dei Carmini (see p38). It makes for a memorable evening.

8 Palazzetto Bru Zane
MAP L2 ■ S Polo 2368 ■ 041 521 10 05 ■ www.bru-zane.com

Housed in the ornate 17th-century Palazzetto Bru Zane, the Centre for French Romantic Music hosts concerts of French chamber music and symphonic and choral works dating between 1780 and 1920. It also organizes lectures and educational activities.

9 Auditorium Santa Margherita
MAP K5 ■ Campo S Margherita, Dorsoduro 3689

This converted church (see p38) sometimes stages world and other music performances for free. Details are generally posted on the door.

A performance at Teatro Goldoni

10 Teatro Goldoni
MAP P4 ■ Calle del Teatro, S Marco 4650/B ■ Ticket sales: 041 240 20 11 ■ www.teatrostabileveneto.it

Teatro Goldoni is one of the oldest theatres in the city, dating from the 17th century. It acquired its present name in 1875 in honour of the 18th-century playwright Carlo Goldoni (see p52). An excellent range of international plays is performed in Italian between November and May.

TOP 10 FILMS SET IN VENICE

Indiana Jones in Venice

1 Indiana Jones and the Last Crusade (1989)
Hero Harrison Ford heaves up the floor in the church of San Barnaba.

2 Summertime (1955)
Single American woman Katharine Hepburn meets an Italian man in Piazza San Marco and falls in love.

3 Death in Venice (1971)
Visconti's film starring Dirk Bogarde is now as classic as the Thomas Mann (see p52) novel on which it is based.

4 Don't Look Now (1973)
This thriller, directed by Nicolas Roeg, with Donald Sutherland and Julie Christie, will keep you awake at night.

5 The Merchant of Venice (2004)
Shakespeare adaptation starring Al Pacino as a brilliant Shylock.

6 Eve (1962)
Joseph Losey's black-and-white classic starring "temptress" Jeanne Moreau.

7 Senso (1954)
Alida Valli betrays family and country for an Austrian officer in another Visconti film.

8 Fellini's Casanova (1976)
Donald Sutherland walks around a fantasized version of Venice in this Fellini film.

9 The Wings of the Dove (1997)
Helena Bonham Carter stars in the film version of Henry James's Venetian story.

10 Casino Royale (2006)
In his first outing as James Bond, Daniel Craig runs the city's alleys and makes a splash in the waterways.

🔟 Pubs, Bars and Clubs

Paradiso Perduto

here – a concert of Irish music in the cosy square, or screens showing rugby and football games. At Carnival and, of course, on St Patrick's Day, this is the place to be.

4 Bacaro Jazz
MAP Q3 ▪ Salizzada Fontego dei Tedeschi, S Marco 5546 ▪ 041 528 52 49

An enthusiastic multilingual welcome is extended to all visitors in this lively wine bar that never seems to close. It boasts almost non-stop service, an extended "happy hour" from 4 to 7pm and a delicious assortment of Spanish-style tapas snack meals to accompany the wine.

1 Paradiso Perduto
MAP D2 ▪ Fondamenta della Misericordia, Cannaregio 2540 ▪ 041 720 581

Call it animated or just plain noisy, but live world music, flowing wine and simple seafood are all part of the vibrant atmosphere at "Paradise Lost". Always packed full to the (low) rafters, the exuberant crowd often spills out onto the canal side where tables are set up in spring and summer months.

2 La Cantina
MAP N1 ▪ Campo San Felice, Cannaregio 3689 ▪ 041 522 82 58 ▪ Closed Sun

This bustling bar specializes in oysters shucked to order and other superbly fresh raw-fish delicacies. There is tasty charcuterie too, and an array of up to 30 wines to order by the glass. Elbow your way to the bar or grab an outside table.

3 The Irish Pub
MAP D2
▪ Campiello dei Testori, Cannaregio 3847
▪ 041 099 01 96

This is a marvellous pub with a lively Celtic atmosphere. You can always count on action

Bacaro Jazz

5 Skyline

MAP B6 ■ Molino Stucky Hilton, Campo San Biagio, Giudecca 810 ■ 041 272 33 11

This bar on the rooftop of the Molino Stucky Hilton hotel is the ultimate spot for a refreshing sundowner. Enjoy a cocktail as you gaze across the canal towards the Zattere, or take a dip in the pool.

6 Casinò Municipale, Palazzo Vendramin-Calergi

MAP C2 ■ Campiello Vendramin, Cannaregio 2040

A magnificent start to an exciting evening – a special ACTV launch from Piazzale Roma transports hopeful clients down the Grand Canal to the landing stage of the beautiful Renaissance palace, alias City Casino, for a glittering night at the tables or the slot machines. It is also a short walk from the San Marcuola ferry stop.

7 Martini Scala-Club Piano Bar

MAP N5 ■ Campo S Fantin, S Marco 1980 ■ Closed Tue ■ 041 522 41 21

This chic locale is the only place in Venice where you can enjoy high-quality cuisine and wine until the small hours of the morning, while being entertained by live music in air-conditioned comfort. No sleeveless tops or shorts, for men or women, are allowed.

8 Osteria da Filo

MAP L2 ■ Calle del Tentor, Santa Croce 1539 ■ 041 524 65 54

This relaxed bar is popular with students, who come for the cold-cut platters and the house wine, or to sip one of the many cocktails on offer. La Poppa, as it is fondly known, is open until 11pm every night.

9 Piccolo Mondo

MAP L6 ■ Calle Contarini Corfù, Dorsoduro 1056/A ■ 041 520 03 71

This tiny club, which does not open until 11pm, has a laid-back atmosphere. The entrance is close to the Accademia Galleries.

10 Le Bistrot de Venise

MAP P4 ■ Calle dei Fabbri, S Marco 4685 ■ 041 523 66 51 ■ Closed 22–25 Dec ■ www.bistrotdevenise.com

An eclectic programme of events here never ceases to entertain, from poetry readings to art exhibitions and wine and food events. An added bonus is superb wine and a fascinating menu of dishes based on traditional 15th-century recipes.

Alfresco dining at Le Bistrot de Venise

🔟 Places to Eat in Venice

Quiet, canal-side dining at Hotel Cipriani

① Hotel Cipriani

Guests are ferried from Piazza San Marco to this hotel restaurant (see p127) in a private launch for a memorable gastronomic experience at two venues, Oro and Cip's Club. The former affords stunning views of the lagoon; the latter fantastic vistas of St Mark's Square. *Tagliolini gratinati al prosciutto* (ribbon pasta with ham, browned in the oven) is a speciality.

② Da Fiore

Reservations are essential at this sophisticated restaurant (see p93), where the owners base the day's menu on what is fresh at the market. They might have *pappardelle con ostriche e zafferano* (flat ribbon pasta with oysters and saffron) or *moleche fritte con polenta* (fried soft-shelled crab with polenta). Excellent use of seasonal produce has made this hidden gem a gourmet heaven.

③ Grand Canal, Hotel Monaco

This restaurant (see p87) serves traditional Venetian and Italian cuisine of a very high standard, including freshly made pasta with shrimp or delicious seafood risotto, accompanied by the best of European wines. The setting, a terrace looking on to the Grand Canal, is stunning.

④ Osteria Boccadoro

Romantically situated beneath a vine-clad pergola, the charming Osteria Boccadoro (see p107) offers creative dishes with delicate flavours and fresh ingredients, such as ribbon pasta with scallops and courgette (zucchini) flowers. Beware the superb *mousse al cioccolato* – it's made with five different kinds of chocolate!

⑤ Corte Sconta

This former *osteria* is now a trendy restaurant (see p113) that serves memorable seafood in a pretty "hidden courtyard" (*corte sconta*). Don't miss the *pincia*, the local bread pudding, for dessert. The house wine is also wonderful. Booking several days in advance is essential for most of the year.

⑥ Do Forni

Customers enter an imitation Orient Express dining car to be greeted by displays of glistening seafood at this award-winning restaurant (see p87) popular with business people, located right by Piazza San Marco. Book ahead.

⑦ Vini da Gigio

The owner prides himself on his Italian and foreign wines to accompany dishes such as *tagliata di tonno* (fresh tuna fillet with herbs) and agnello (lamb) at this tiny well-established restaurant *(see p107)* with a great reputation. Booking is recommended.

8 La Bitta

The cosy, rustic La Bitta *(see p101)* specializes in succulent meat dishes served with seasonal vegetables and superb wines. The innovative menu changes almost every day according to market availability and never includes fish.

9 Osteria di Santa Marina

Seafood is the star of the menu at this elegant restaurant *(see p113)*; the baby octopus with red onion and orange is highly recommended. There is a wonderful six-course tasting menu of Venetian specialities. The wine list is impressive too.

10 Trattoria alla Madonna

This popular restaurant *(see p87)* is the perfect place for traditional dishes such as delicate *granseola* (spider crab). An inspiring display of fresh seafood, such as *spaghetti con nero* (with cuttlefish ink sauce) and *anguilla fritta* (fried eel), is available here as well. It is not possible to make a reservation, so expect to queue.

Trattoria alla Madonna

TOP 10 VENETIAN DISHES

Tiramisù, a classic Italian dessert

1 Tiramisù
Dessert with a creamy sauce of eggs and mascarpone between layers of sponge drenched in coffee or liqueur.

2 Carpaccio
Raw beef sliced thin and sprinkled with rocket *(rucola)* or flakes of Parmesan cheese.

3 Sarde in Saor
Fried sardines marinated in a sweet-and-sour mixture of onions, currants and pine nuts, invented for sailors at sea for lengthy periods.

4 Antipasto di Frutti di Mare
Seafood platter of baby octopus, anchovies, shrimp or whatever else is in season.

5 Prosciutto e Melone
The sweetness of wedges of fresh rock melon is contrasted with the slightly salty cured Parma ham.

6 Risotto di Pesce
Clams, mussels, shrimp and assorted fish in a heavenly creamy rice dish.

7 Pasta con il Nero di Seppia
Usually spaghetti, combined with a rich sauce of tomato and cuttlefish, thoroughly blackened with the ink.

8 Fegato alla Veneziana
Venetian-style calves' liver cooked slowly with onions and vinegar.

9 Grilled Fish
Such as *coda di rospo* (monkfish) or *pesce spada* (swordfish) from the south.

10 Grilled Vegetables
Radicchio (red chicory) in winter, *zucchine* (courgettes) and *melanzane* (aubergine/eggplant) in summer, and roasted *peperoni* (peppers).

Osterie (Wine Bars)

Cantina Do Mori

1 Cantina Do Mori
MAP N2 ■ Calle dei Do Mori, S Polo 429

Rows of copper polenta pots hang overhead in this dark, popular bar, billed as the city's oldest *osteria*. The affable owners pour wine directly from huge demijohns and serve delicate postage-stamp-sized ham and salad sandwiches *(francobolli)*.

2 Un Mondo diVino
MAP E3 ■ Salizzada S Canciano, Cannaregio 5984A

Italian wines can be enjoyed at this converted butcher's shop, along with mouthwatering bar snacks such as *insalata di mare* (seafood salad) and regional cheeses. This place is well frequented by both locals and visitors, who spill out from the bar and into the alleyway, glass in hand.

3 Osteria Ruga Rialto
MAP N3 ■ Ruga Vecchia S Giovanni, S Polo 692A

Verging on rowdy, this traditional establishment turns out crisp mounds of fried calamari and vegetables at evening *aperitivo* time, when you'll have to elbow your way past the locals to reach the bar. Lunch and dinner are somewhat quieter affairs.

4 Osteria del Sacro e Profano
MAP P2 ■ Ramo secondo del Parangon, S Polo 502

Well worth hunting out near Rialto, this rustic-looking *osteria* is the haunt of international artists, who happily mingle with the locals. Wines from the Veneto and Friuli are served with traditional snacks such as *uova con acciughe* (hard-boiled egg with anchovy).

5 Vinus Venezia
MAP K4 ■ Calle del Scalater Rocco, Dorsoduro 3961

This stylish wine bar serves a fantastic range of local and national wines, accompanied by elegant bar snacks made from locally produced ingredients, such as artichoke crostini.

6 Enoteca do Colonne
MAP C2 ■ Rio Terrà del Cristo, Cannaregio 1814C

All manner of counter food *(cicchetti)*, ranging from *baccalà* (salted cod) on crusty bread to hearty *musetto* sausage, is served with great smiles by the affable young owners at this lively neighbourhood bar. There's a also a good selection of Veneto wines.

Food counter at Enoteca do Colonne

7 Osteria alla Frasca
MAP E2 ■ Corte della Carità, Cannaregio 5176

Said to be the site where Titian kept his paints and canvases, this is now a tiny picturesque bar serving drinks and snacks on a vine-covered terrace in summer.

8 Trattoria Antico Calice
MAP Q3 ■ Calle dei Stagneri, S Marco 5228

You have to fight your way through the locals here, attracted by the lively atmosphere and counter overflowing with local wines and appetizing snacks such as fried sardines in breadcrumbs.

9 Trattoria Ca' d'Oro alla Vedova
MAP D2 ■ Calle del Pistor, Cannaregio 3912

A young and enterprising team runs this timber-panelled venue, which has been serving mouthwatering *cicchetti*, such as crispy battered artichokes and meatballs *(polpetti)*, along with quaffable wine, for longer than any of the regulars can remember. There are also main dishes, served at tables.

Exterior of Al Bottegon

10 Al Bottegon
MAP C5 ■ Fondamenta Nani, Dorsoduro 992

Join the locals at this family-run specialist wine cellar, located not far from the Accademia Bridge, for excellent Prosecco at the stand-up bar. Simple nibbles to accompany the wine include *mortadella* sausage and *panini* filled with *sopressa*, a local salami.

TOP 10 DRINKS

Refreshing Spritz al Bitter

1 Spritz
Venetian favourite of white wine with a splash of Bitter, Aperol or Select *(aperitivo* brands) and a shot of mineral water.

2 Prosecco
Excellent, sparkling, dry white wine from the hills around Conegliano and Valdobbiadene.

3 Bellini
Smooth fresh peach juice and sparkling Prosecco blend, invented by Cipriani of Harry's Bar (Calle Vallaresso, S Marco 1323, *see p25*).

4 Red Wine
An *ombra* means a small glass of house wine, otherwise try quality Cabernet, Valpolicella or Amarone.

5 White Wine
Soave and Pinot Grigio are worthwhile alternatives to house varieties.

6 Mineral Water
Widely consumed in Italy, either sparkling *(con gas)* or still *(senza gas)*. Tap water is *acqua dal rubinetto*.

7 Fruit Drinks
These can be ordered as *spremuta* (freshly squeezed juice) or *succo di frutta* (bottled nectars).

8 Coffee
Straight espresso, frothy cappuccino or *caffè latte* in a tall glass with hot milk.

9 Hot Chocolate
Usually served in the winter months. An *espresso* milk-free version can be found in good chocolate emporia.

10 After-dinner Sgroppino
A well-kept local secret concocted with lemon sorbet, vodka and Prosecco.

🔟 Shops in Venice

1 Ca' Macana
MAP K6 ■ Calle delle Botteghe, Dorsoduro 3172

Buy one of Venice's famous papier-mâché masks at this shop, which carries the full Carnival range and much more besides. You can watch the mask-makers in action or even attend a course in making or painting your own.

2 Nardi
MAP Q5 ■ Piazza S Marco 69, S Marco

Elizabeth Taylor, Grace Kelly and Elton John have all happily spent time (and more) in this plush boutique of glittering marvels. Three generations of craftsmen have thrilled those who can afford it with breathtaking pieces, such as their blackamoor brooch in ruby and gold or diamond and platinum.

3 Luigi Bevilacqua
MAP L2 ■ Campiello della Comare, S Croce 1320

Shimmering velvets, silks and damasks are fashioned into wonderful bags, clothes and shoes. The Bevilacqua family has been weaving precious fabrics by hand since the 1700s and you can see the ancient looms they continue to use today (see also p85).

4 Venini
MAP Q4 ■ Piazzetta Leoncini, S Marco 314

Don't expect Venetian glass animals here, rather innovative platters and vases of great simplicity and style. Since its 1921 beginnings, Venini's award-winning design team has included top names Carlo Scarpa and Gae Aulenti.

5 Attombri
MAP P3 ■ Sottoportico degli Orefici, S Polo 65

Beautifully crafted bead jewellery is made on the premises by brothers Stefano and Daniele. Pieces range from delicate earrings to in-your-face flamboyant necklaces.

Colourful pasta at Rizzo

6 Rizzo
MAP Q2 ■ Salizzada S Giovanni Crisostomo, Cannaregio 5778

Jet-black tagliatelle ribbons coloured with cuttlefish ink are just one option out of more than 40 imaginative pasta shapes that can be found on sale at Rizzo. Mouthwatering handmade chocolates and multicoloured Carnival masks also make marvellous souvenirs to take home.

7 T Fondaco dei Tedeschi
MAP P3 ■ Calle del Fontego dei Tedeschi, Rialto Bridge, 30124

Originally used as a warehouse and lodgings for German traders,

Ancient looms at Luigi Bevilacqua

this old building has now been completely refurbished as a popular luxury department store. The lovely rooftop terrace is known for its stunning views.

8 Rubelli
MAP M4 ■ **Campiello del Teatro, S Marco 3877**

Venice's past contact with the Orient is conjured up by the sumptuous handmade furnishings in this show-room. A blend of computer technology and traditional techniques is used for the brocades, damasks and silks.

Wide range of paper at Paolo Olbi

9 Paolo Olbi
MAP N4 ■ **Dorsoduro 3253/A**

This shop contains exquisite photo albums and address books in rainbow-coloured marbled paper and leather. All at reasonable prices, they are made by one of the original craftsmen in Venice.

10 Signor Blum

The meticulously hand-crafted and hand-painted wooden items on display in this corner store *(see p100)*, make for original presents and sou-venirs. The range includes pictures of the city's landmark buildings and portraits of outstanding musicians as fridge magnets.

TOP 10 SOUVENIRS

Murano glassware

1 Glassware
Impress your guests back home with a genuine Murano chandelier or perhaps a *millefiori* paperweight.

2 Gourmet Food
For something authentically Italian but intrinsically Venetian, try extra virgin olive oil flavoured with chilli peppers, bottled red chicory paste or pasta in the shape of gondolas and masks.

3 T-shirts
The essential guaranteed souvenir of Venice, sold at the ubiquitous street stalls.

4 Masks
A mind-boggling array of masks, traditionally made for Carnival in papier-mâché, ceramic and even leather.

5 Marbled Paper
Swirls of pastel hues can be used for covering books or simply as elegant wrapping paper for gifts.

6 Beads
All manner of beads, from frosted glass to ceramic or the traditional, colourful murrhine mosaic-style, can be found.

7 Italian Wine and Liqueurs
Take advantage of lower prices and taxes by stocking up on locally produced wines.

8 Fabric
Lace is the most Venetian of materials, but attractive linens and velvets are also good value.

9 Silverwork
Photo frames, letter openers and teaspoons make lovely gifts for friends.

10 Clothes
All the top fashion names can be found in Venice.

Venice for Free

Mosaics in the Basilica di San Marco

1 Basilica di San Marco

Entry to the city's main church (see pp12–13), plastered with glittering Byzantine mosaics, is free of charge. Modelled on Saint Sophia in Constantinople, the basilica is a glorious reflection of the city's Byzantine connection. The cavernous building has walls lined with artistically cut rock-slabs and superb geometric patterns on the floor.

2 Take a Free Walking Tour

www.venicefreewalkingtour.com

Every morning and afternoon, free guided walking tours in English are organized from Campo Santi Apostoli in Cannaregio. Knowledgeable volunteers accompany visitors on short walks through places off the beaten track. It is essential to book ahead to ensure a place.

3 Art Night

www.artnightvenezia.it

Concerts, exhibitions, lectures, demonstrations of craft techniques, and videos are on all over the city on a set night in June (see the website), all organized by the City Council and Ca' Foscari University. Reservations are necessary for some events.

4 Free Museum Entry

On the first Sunday of each month, entry to all Italian state-run museums and galleries is free for all visitors. In Venice, this includes the Gallerie dell'Accademia, Galleria Franchetti alla Ca' d'Oro, Museo Archeologico, Museo d'Arte Orientale and Palazzo Grimani.

5 Watching the Boats Go By

Settle down on any canal edge, and enjoy the unique sight of people going about their day-to-day business by boat – rubbish barges, transport floats, florist boats, taxi launches, to mention a few. And the water is often shared by ducks and cormorants fishing. Choice spots are Punta della Dogana (see p98), the Zattere (see p97) and the main Cannaregio canal.

6 T Fondaco dei Tedeschi Rooftop Terrace

MAP P3 ▪ Calle del Fontego dei Tedeschi, Rialto Bridge, S Marco ▪ 041 314 20 00 ▪ Open daily (times vary) ▪ www.dfs.com

Located at the foot of the Rialto Bridge, this modern department store is housed in the former main post office building, which has been transformed into luxury shops. The top of the building affords spectacular views – book a free visit online.

7 Museo della Musica

MAP N6 ▪ Chiesa di S Maurizio, Campo S Maurizio, S Marco ▪ 041 241 18 40

This fascinating museum in converted church premises offers free entrance, allowing visitors to admire its historical collection of remarkable musical instruments dating back to the time of Vivaldi.

Museo della Musica

8 Isola di San Michele Cemetery

An island circled by tall brick walls and dotted with cypress trees houses the city's monumental cemetery (see p118). Even if you have little interest in paying homage at the tombs of notable residents Igor Stravinsky, Diaghilev or Joseph Brodsky, it's a pleasant spot simply for strolling around.

Isola di San Michele Cemetery

9 Castello Giardini Pubblici

Over in the Castello district, these gardens were laid out in the late 1800s by the French occupiers, as quickly becomes clear from the style. Shade and benches can be enjoyed to rest your weary feet, while the children let off steam in the playground (see p111).

Castello Giardini Pubblici

10 Free Concerts

In churches and neighbourhood halls, orchestras and choirs from Italy and overseas often hold concerts, which are free to spectators. To find out about these events in advance, check the street posters affixed to the city walls.

TOP 10 MONEY-SAVING TIPS

Avoiding café service charges

1 To avoid the waiter service charge at cafés, do as the locals do and take your drink at the bar instead of sitting down at a table.

2 For cheap accommodation search for last-minute deals online.

3 A house exchange is a low-cost way to experience Venice – and to live as the locals live.

4 Admire masterpieces – paintings and sculptures – in the city's many churches, where admission charges are modest.

5 Buy a slice of pizza at one of the many *pizza al taglio* establishments. It's the perfect food option when you're on the go.

6 Buy picnic supplies at a supermarket, and fill up your water bottle at a tap or fountain. For picnic areas see #EnjoyRespectVenezia at www.comune.venezia.it

7 Purchase a Venezia Unica pass in advance online (www.veneziaunica.it). You can use this for ferries and sightseeing, saving both queuing time and money.

8 During the Biennale art event (every two years; www.labiennale.org), visit the many free shows that are dotted around the city.

9 Cheap fashion clothes and shoes are on sale at the weekly markets on the Lido on Tuesday.

10 The Rolling Venice card (www.veneziaunica.it) offers discounted rates at shops and restaurants for young visitors (those aged 6–29).

Festivals and Events

1 Carnival
Feb–Mar, concluding on Shrove Tue, 40 days before Easter

This unmissable 10-day extravaganza takes over the city as a countdown to Lent. The streets mill with costumed and masked local "nobility" or crazily attired visitors. It gets off to a flying start with the Volo dell'Angelo (flight of the angel), when either an acrobat or a cardboard dove is launched from the Campanile in Piazza San Marco, showering onlookers with confetti. The grand finale is the explosive Mardi Gras.

Carnival-goer in full costume

2 Su e Zo per i Ponti
Late Mar/Apr: 4th Sun in Lent

Anyone can join this leisurely non-competitive walk or run "up and down the bridges". Several official routes can be followed, and all participants receive a medal on finishing.

3 Festa della Sensa
May: Ascension Day

Head for the Riviera di San Nicolò at the Lido (see p123) to watch this ancient ceremony of "Venice wedding to the Sea". A costumed "doge" casts a ring into the sea amid a procession of celebratory boats. Symbolizing Venice's maritime supremacy, La Sensa has been staged since Venice took Istria and Dalmatia in AD 997.

4 Vogalonga
May: Sun after Ascension

A colourful armada of rowing craft from all over the world embarks on a 32-km (20-mile) non-competitive route around the lagoon's scattered islands. The "Long Row" is a great experience for both participants and onlookers, who line the Canale di Cannaregio towards midday to cheer on the breathtaking final stretch down the Grand Canal.

5 Biennale Art Exhibition
Jun–Nov

The world's leading international art bonanza is held on a two-yearly basis. The leafy gardens in eastern Castello are the principal venue, supplemented by the Corderie building in the Arsenale.

6 Festa del Redentore
Mid-Jul

People crowd on to all available watercraft, decorated with paper lanterns and greenery, for a feast of roast duck and watermelon, followed by a midnight fireworks display. It all takes place near Palladio's church on

Midnight fireworks on Festa del Redentore

Giudecca *(see p123)* to commemorate the end of the 1576 plague. For those getting there on foot, a temporary pontoon bridge stretches from the Zattere over the Giudecca canal.

7 Festa di San Rocco
16 Aug

The feast day of St Roch, the French saint adopted by the confraternity for alleviating the 1576–7 plague, is celebrated each year at the Scuola Grande di San Rocco *(see p89)*.

Colourful boats at Regata Storica

8 Regata Storica
1st Sun in Sep

The word regatta originated in Venice, so what better place to enjoy the year's most spectacular event. Ornately decorated boats propelled by costumed oarsmen parade down the Grand Canal bearing passengers dressed as historical dignitaries. A series of furiously contested regattas follows.

9 Venice Marathon
Late Oct

Runners from all parts of the globe begin this classic – not to mention beautiful – 42-km (26-mile) race at Villa Pisani on the Brenta waterway, cross the causeway to Venice, the Zattere and San Marco, and finish near the public gardens in Castello.

10 Festa della Salute
21 Nov

Venetians make a pilgrimage to Longhena's church *(see p48)* every winter in memory of the devastating plague of 1630–31. The whole area assumes a festive atmosphere with stalls selling candy floss and balloons.

TOP 10 SPORTS IN VENICE

A women's rowing team, practising on the waterways of Venice

1 Rowing
MAP D5 ▪ Zattere, Dorsoduro
Immensely popular Venetian pastime practised standing up. Join the oldest club, Canottieri Bucintoro.

2 Cycling
MAP H2 ▪ Gran Viale SM Elisabetta
Illegal in Venice itself, though you'll see kids zooming around. It is allowed in Lido, where you can rent a bike from a cycle shop on the main street.

3 Sailing
Yachtsmen gather at the marina on San Giorgio Maggiore island.

4 Swimming
Head for the Lido, or the crowded indoor pools at Sacca Fisola and Sant'Alvise.

5 In-Line Skating
There is a small rink at Sant'Elena in Castello, otherwise stick to the Lido *(see p123)* pavements.

6 Golf
MAP H2 ▪ Strada Vecchia, 1
The well-reputed 18-hole course at the Alberoni is on the south of the Lido.

7 Tennis
MAP H2 ▪ Lungomare G Marconi 41/D
The Lido has the only courts available to visitors.

8 Jogging
The city's stone paving doesn't do wonders for your knees, so try the city parks.

9 Gyms
Private gyms with state-of-the-art equipment can be found online.

10 Football
MAP H2 ▪ Stadio Pierluigi Penzo
The home team Venezia plays at Sant'Elena stadium on Sundays.

Venice
Area by Area

Lungo and Rio di San Trovaso, Dorsoduro

🔟 San Marco

Venice's smallest but foremost *sestiere* (district), named after the city's patron saint, is bounded by the Grand Canal on all but one side, which explains the number of stately palaces in the area. It revolves around Piazza San Marco and the majestic Doge's Palace *(see pp16–19)*, the political and legal core of the city until the 18th century. Running off the square are the Mercerie and Calle Larga XXII Marzo, offering wall-to-wall designer shopping. But beyond that San Marco has a residential air, with a great range of places to eat. Don't hesitate to wander down minor alleyways: surprises include unusual wellheads and many craft workshops.

Niccolò Tommaseo

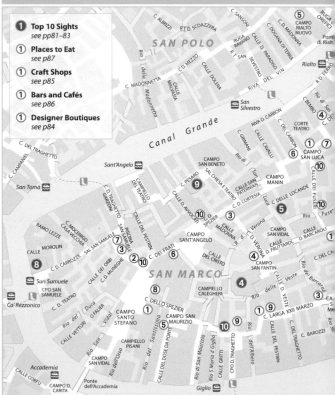

SAN MARCO

1 **Top 10 Sights**
see pp81–83

1 **Places to Eat**
see p87

1 **Craft Shops**
see p85

1 **Bars and Cafés**
see p86

1 **Designer Boutiques**
see p84

1 Piazza San Marco
See pp20–23.

2 Mercerie
MAP Q4

The expensive elegance of Venice is most evident on this main thoroughfare linking Rialto and Piazza San Marco. *Mercerie* means haberdasher's, but these days it is home to designer fashion outlets. Just below the ornate Torre dell'Orologio archway is a sculpted female figure commemorating a housewife who lived here rent-free as a reward for inadvertently knocking a mortar into the street, killing a revolutionary leader and so halting the short-lived Bajamonte Tiepolo revolt in 1310.

3 Basilica di San Marco

Built on a Greek cross plan, and crowned with five huge domes, this is the third church *(see pp12–15)* to stand on this site. In 1807, it succeeded San Pietro in Castello as the cathedral of Venice. Dark, mysterious and enriched with the spoils of conquest, the basilica is a unique blend of Eastern and Western influences. Embellished over a period of six centuries, it features fabulous mosaics, marble and carvings and served as a fitting location for ceremonies of the Republic. It was here that the elected doge was presented to the city following his election. This is also where sea captains came to pray for protection before embarking on epic voyages.

4 Teatro La Fenice
MAP N5 ■ **Campo S Fantin**
■ **Daily guided tours**

Long masked in scaffolding since a 1996 arson attack left it gutted, the historic "Phoenix" theatre rose from the flames in 2003. Selva's 1792 opera house has staged countless world premieres including Rossini's *Tancredi* in 1813, five operas commissioned of Verdi, most notably *Rigoletto* and *La Traviata*, and works by Stravinsky and Luigi Nono. Legendary divas such as Maria Callas and Dame Joan Sutherland have sung in this glorious setting *(see p62)*.

Concert at Teatro La Fenice

5 Scala Contarini del Bovolo

MAP P4 ■ Corte dei Risi, S Marco 4299
■ Open 10am–6pm daily ■ Adm
■ www.scalacontarinidelbovolo.com

Often used as a film set, this fine 15th-century palace with its beautiful external "snail-shell" staircase (*bovolo* means snail in Venetian) is squeezed into a diminutive square deep in San Marco. Visitors can climb the winding steps of the staircase, a blend of Renaissance, Gothic and Byzantine styles, via five floors of loggias to a dome sheltering a splendid belvedere. From here there are magical panoramic views over the city's rooftops.

GLASSMAKING

Venetian glasswork exquisitely decorates chandeliers, chalices and mirrors and has long been in demand the world over, especially during the Golden Age of the 16th century. Although the industry moved to Murano (**above**) in 1295 as a safety measure against fire, there are still many furnaces around the San Marco district that welcome visitors.

6 Campo San Bartolomeo

MAP P3

The statue of celebrated Venetian playwright Carlo Goldoni scrutinizes the milling crowds on this crossroads square. Strategically placed for a host of inviting bars crammed into the alleys radiating off it, "San Bartolo" serves as the fashionable hang-out for the city's young and trendy. The northern end is occupied by the main post office, once home to Venice's German community (*see p51*). They worshipped in the Chiesa di San Bartolomeo (open 10am–noon Tue, Thu & Sat; free admission).

Carlo Goldoni

7 Doge's Palace

The seat of the Venetian government from the 9th century until the fall of the Republic in 1797, the Doge's Palace (*see pp16–17*) was the official residence of the Venetian ruler, known as the doge. It started life as a fortified castle in the 9th century, but this and several subsequent buildings were destroyed by a series of fires. A Gothic masterpiece, the bulk of the pink marble building appears perched on loggias and arcades of white Istrian stone.

Allegorical historical paintings embellish the walls and ceilings of the halls and chambers. These rooms are testament to the glory of the Venetian Republic.

8 Palazzo Grassi

MAP L5 ■ Campo S Samuele, S Marco 3231 ■ Open 10am–7pm Wed–Mon ■ Adm (includes Punta della Dogana) ■ www.palazzograssi.it

Set on the Grand Canal, Palazzo Grassi (*see p54*) dates back to 1740, when a wealthy merchant family commissioned Giorgio Massari to design the building. It is now home to the François Pinault collection, housing contemporary masterpieces by Jeff Koons, Damien Hirst and Michelangelo Pistoletto. It stands alongside picturesque Campo San Samuele, which features a graceful Veneto-Byzantine bell tower.

9 Museo Fortuny

MAP N4 ■ Campo S Benedetto, S Marco 3780 ■ Open 10am–6pm Wed–Mon ■ Adm ■ www.visitmuve.it

Flamboyant Spanish artist and theatrical stage designer Mariano Fortuny y Madrazo (1871–1950) adopted Venice as his home and muse, and transformed this

15th-century palace in Gothic-Venetian style into an exotic atelier. The building retains rooms created by Fortuny himself and visitors can admire Fortuny's gorgeous velvets, his famous pleated silk dresses, some 150 paintings, lamps, a remarkable stage curtain and fascinating 19th-century photographs. The museum also hosts temporary exhibitions.

Museo Fortuny

⑩ Chiesa di Santa Maria del Giglio

MAP N6 ■ Campo S Maria del Giglio, S Marco 3231 ■ Open 10:30am–4:30pm Mon–Sat ■ Adm ■ www.chorusvenezia.org

Opening on to a lovely square next to the Grand Canal, this church is a further example of Venetian Baroque extravagance. Commissioned by the Barbaro family, its façade exalts their generations of maritime and political triumphs, with crests, galleys and statues. Works of art inside the church include Venice's only canvas by Rubens, depicting a Madonna and child. Tintoretto's contributions are the Evangelists on the organ doors.

Ceiling fresco in the Chiesa di Santa Maria del Giglio

A DAY IN SAN MARCO

▶ MORNING

Visit the **Doge's Palace** on Piazza San Marco first, arriving early to fit it all in. Must-sees are the Sala del Senato, Sala del Maggior Consiglio, prisons and the Bridge of Sighs. Then take a break for coffee in the modern café in the palace's former stables and watch the gondolas glide past the glassed-in doorway.

Time your visit to **Basilica di San Marco** (see p81) for midday, to catch the mosaics illuminated by huge spotlights so they glitter to their utmost. The tiles were laid at angles to catch the light.

Lunch at **Harry's Bar**, as Hemingway's hero did in *Across the River and into the Trees*. Order the *carpaccio* (wafer-thin slices of raw beef) invented here by Cipriani (see p25).

AFTERNOON

The **Mercerie** (see p81) is shopper's heaven, packed with international high-fashion stores from Benetton to Cartier, and classy souvenir glass and hand-crafted paper workshops. For yet more, cross over to **Calle Larga XXII Marzo** for designer delights such as **Bulgari** and **Cartier** jewellery (see p84).

Return to **Piazza San Marco** (see pp20–23) in time to enjoy the views over Venice and the lagoon from the Campanile at dusk. At ground level again, it's time for a Bellini *aperitivo* at **Caffè Florian** (see p21) to watch the sun set over the façade of the basilica.

See map on pp80–81

Designer Boutiques

(1) Frette
MAP P5 ■ Frezzeria,
S Marco 1725

Since 1860, Frette has been importing top-grade cotton from Egypt and transforming it into towels and custom-made household linen.

L'Isola – Carlo Moretti

(2) L'Isola – Carlo Moretti
MAP M5 ■ Calle delle
Botteghe, S Marco 2970

Exhibited in galleries all over the world, this is contemporary glass at its most innovative. Moretti's trademarks are "paper cone" vases, tumblers and huge sculptures.

(3) Marina e Susanna Sent
MAP P5 ■ Ponte S Moisè,
S Marco 2090

Come here for strikingly simple but exquisitely elegant necklaces and earrings in clear and coloured glass designed by two sisters.

(4) Ottico Fabbricatore
MAP P3 ■ Calle dell'Ovo,
S Marco 4773

This small store offers an array of exclusive designer glasses with frames made from buffalo horn and titanium, as well as blown-glass vases and lamps. You can also get cashmere clothing in 70 colours and luxury bags in various leathers.

(5) Cartier
MAP P5 ■ Calle San Moisè,
S Marco 1474

The fortress-like premises of these world-famous French jewellers gleam with gold, precious stones and well-crafted handbags and watches.

(6) MaxMara
MAP P3 ■ Campo S Salvador,
S Marco 5033

This family company has been designing fashionable clothes and accessories for city girls since 1951.

(7) Bulgari
MAP P5 ■ Salizzada San Moisè,
S Marco 1494

Striking contemporary jewellery, watches, accessories and Rosenthal porcelain are sold here.

(8) Fratelli Rossetti
MAP P3 ■ Campo S Salvador,
S Marco 4800

This family-run firm was established in 1953 and is known worldwide for the superb Italian elegance it displays in the likes of shoes, belts, bags and jackets.

(9) Fendi
MAP P5 ■ Frezzeria,
S Marco 1582

Go straight to the source for flamboyant frocks and shoes for special occasions and crazily beaded bags, all sporting the "double-F" Fendi mark.

(10) Arnoldo e Battois
MAP P4 ■ Calle dei Fuseri,
S Marco 4271

Fabulous Italian fashion is available here from designers Silvano Arnoldo and Massimiliano Battois – let them help you create your look in this minimalist cube of a store.

Arnoldo e Battois
shoulder bag

Craft Shops

1 Venetia Studium
MAP P5 ■ Calle Larga XXII Marzo, S Marco 2425

Exquisite hanging silk lamps of Fortuny design are reproduced with hand-painted patterning and glass beading.

2 Legatoria La Fenice
MAP Q4 ■ Campiello della Feltrina, S Marco 826

Right off Piazza San Marco, this artisanal workshop has stationery, printed paper and books bound in leather, all crafted by hand.

3 BAC Art Studio
MAP M5 ■ Calle delle Botteghe, S Marco 3451

This art gallery sells attractive and affordable etchings and prints of Venice by artists Baruffaldi and Cadore.

4 Max Art
MAP P5 ■ Frezzeria, S Marco 1232

Commedia dell'arte marionettes, musical puppet theatres and glittering Carnival masks are available here for sale or hire.

5 Galleria Livio De Marchi
MAP M6 ■ Calle Dose da Ponte, S Marco 2742

Crumpled boots and a raincoat slung over a chair are actually sculptures – there are even life-size wooden cars, complete with engines.

6 Rigattieri
MAP M5 ■ Calle dei Frati, S Marco 3532/36

Ceramics enthusiasts must not miss this extraordinary shop of beautiful pottery. It has been run by the same family since it was founded – at this address – in 1938, and the focus is firmly on high-quality pieces.

Venetia Studium copper-leaf free-standing lamp

7 Valese Fonditore
MAP Q4 ■ Calle Fiubera, S Marco 793

The Valese family foundry has been creating their animals, lamps and door knockers in brass and bronze since 1913. Examples of their work can even be found in Buckingham Palace and The White House.

8 Le Botteghe della Solidarietà
MAP P3 ■ Salizzada Pio X, S Marco 5164

A kaleidoscopic display of handwoven shawls from India and musical instruments from African countries are part of an enterprise that is intended to guarantee artisans a just income.

9 Bevilacqua
MAP N5 ■ Campo S Maria del Giglio, S Marco 2520

Handmade velvet and silk cushions and tapestries are a feast for the eyes at this small branch of the historic Italian fabric shop *(see also p72)*.

Bevilacqua fabric shop

10 Daniela Ghezzo Segalin a Venezia
MAP P4 ■ Calle dei Fuseri, S Marco 4365

In addition to the brocade slippers and bizarre footwear with built-in toes, special-order shoes are also hand-crafted here.

See map on pp80–81

Bars and Cafés

1 Pasticceria Marchini Time

MAP P4 ■ Campo S Luca, S Marco 4589

A paradise for those with a sweet tooth, Marchini is one of the oldest *pasticcerie* in the city. Orange and pistachio chocolates come in Venetian mask shapes.

2 I Rusteghi
MAP Q3 ■ Corte del Tintor, S Marco 5513 ■ Closed Sun

Tucked away behind Campo San Bartolomeo, this is a cosy *osteria* run by a friendly sommelier-owner. It has an excellent selection of wines and *cicchetti* (bar snacks).

3 Caffè Brasilia

MAP N4 ■ Rio Terrà Assassini, S Marco 3658

Tuck into a huge, fresh fruit salad smothered with yogurt or a *tramezzino* (sandwich) in this quiet side-alley café, with tables inside and a few outside. The coffee's good, too.

4 Bar al Teatro
MAP N5 ■ Campo S Fantin, S Marco 1916

Next door to the renowned Fenice Theatre *(see p81)*, this legendary venue offers outdoor seating on a patio. Alternatively, go inside to the bar and munch a toasted sandwich.

Bar al Teatro

5 Devil's Forest Pub

MAP Q3 ■ Calle dei Stagneri, S Marco 5185

Sporting an original red London phone box, this "English pub" serves draught beers and ales, and light meals until midnight. There is even a dartboard and live music.

6 Bacarando
MAP P3 ■ Corte dell'Orso, S Marco 5495

This great spot offers bar snacks at *aperitivo* time, but also has an elegant restaurant. Wednesday nights see the addition of live music.

Lime cocktail at Bacarando

7 Caffeteria Doria
MAP P4 ■ Calle dei Fabbri, S Marco 4578/C

A friendly, standing-only corner bar, Cafetteria Doria serves divinely rich hot chocolate that is perfect for winter, and refreshing *sorbetto al caffè* in the summer months. There is also an impressive choice of teas.

8 Le Café
MAP M5 ■ Campo S Stefano, S Marco 2797

Have a fresh orange juice or cappuccino and pastry as you watch life go by in the square. The usual hot dishes are available, and there is also a *pasticceria* offering tasty tarts and pastries.

9 Rosa Salva
MAP Q4 ■ Ponte Ferai, S Marco 950

Come here to enjoy melt-in-the-mouth fruit tarts, exquisite pastries and Venice's best panettone.

10 Bar all'Angolo
MAP M5 ■ Campo Santo Stefano, S Marco 3464 ■ Closed Sun

Tourists and locals alike are unable to resist this great sandwich bar. Bag a table outside for a well-earned coffee or light lunch.

Places to Eat

PRICE CATEGORIES

For a three-course meal for one with half a bottle of wine (or equivalent meal), taxes and extra charges.

€ under €40 ■ €€ €40–60 ■ €€€ over €60

1 Ristorante A Beccafico
MAP M5 ■ Campo S Stefano, S Marco 2801 ■ 041 527 48 79 ■ €€€

The menu at this marvellous eatery blends Sicilian dishes with Venetian cuisine and includes pasta, meat and fish, plus fabulous desserts.

2 Grand Canal
MAP Q6 ■ Calle Vallaresso, S Marco 1325 ■ 041 520 02 11 ■ €€€

Part of Hotel Monaco, Grand Canal (see p68) offers stylish dining all year round. The extensive menu features Venetian cuisine and fish dishes.

3 Do Forni
MAP Q4 ■ Calle Specchieri, S Marco, 468 ■ 041 523 21 48 ■ €€€

This elegant restaurant (see p68) boasts a long list of celebrity guests. The menu features seasonal specialities and an extensive wine list.

4 Rosticceria San Bartolomeo
MAP P3 ■ Calle della Bissa, S Marco 5424 ■ 041 522 35 69 ■ €

Also known as the Gislon, this place serves great *mozzarella in carozza*, a deep-fried cheese sandwich.

5 Trattoria alla Madonna
MAP P3 ■ Calle delle Madonna, S Polo 594 ■ 041 522 38 24 ■ Closed Wed, 25 Dec–31 Jan ■ €€

A well-known, bustling restaurant (see p69), perfect for traditional sea-food. Seafood risotto is a speciality.

6 Leon Bianco
MAP P4 ■ Campo S Luca, S Marco 4153 ■ 041 522 11 80 ■ Closed Sat & Sun ■ €

A great spot for grilled meats and fish or lasagne. You have the choice of eating at the bar or at a table out-side. American Express is not accepted.

7 Al Bacareto
MAP M5 ■ Calle delle Botteghe, S Marco 3447 ■ 041 528 93 36 ■ Closed Sun, Aug ■ €

A Venetian stalwart since 1971, Al Bacareto serves typical local dishes. Try the *bigoli in salsa* (spaghetti with anchovy and onion purée).

8 Osteria San Marco
MAP P5 ■ Frezzeria, S Marco 1610 ■ 041 528 52 42 ■ Closed Sun ■ €€

An exemplary wine list accompanies the tasty bar snacks and a small, but perfectly formed, menu.

9 La Caravella
MAP P5 ■ Via XXII Marzo, S Marco 2398 ■ 041 520 89 01 ■ €€€

Resembling a caravel sailing ship, this restaurant has trestle tables adorned with pewter plates. The menu features Venetian dishes with a modern twist and a good wine list.

La Caravella

10 Acqua Pazza
MAP N5 ■ Campo Sant'Angelo, S Marco 3808/10 ■ 041 277 06 88 ■ Closed Mon, 7 Jan–7 Feb ■ €€€

Amalfi cuisine, including Neapolitan pizza, pasta and fish dishes, feature at this fine-dining restaurant.

See map on pp80–81

🔟 San Polo and Santa Croce

Venice's greatest concentration of sights can be found in these neighbouring districts, at the geographical heart of Venice, having grown around the ancient core of Rialto where the first inhabitants settled. Here, glorious churches, landmark monuments and breathtaking palaces are all saturated in history. Essential sights include Santa Maria Gloriosa dei Frari *(see pp32–3)*, the Scuola Grande di San Rocco, where Tintoretto demonstrated his genius on sumptuous canvases, and the morning bustle of Rialto market. The squares of San Polo and San Giacomo dell'Orio are both full of cafés and benches for resting weary feet.

Campo San Giacomo dell'Orio

SAN POLO AND SANTA CROCE

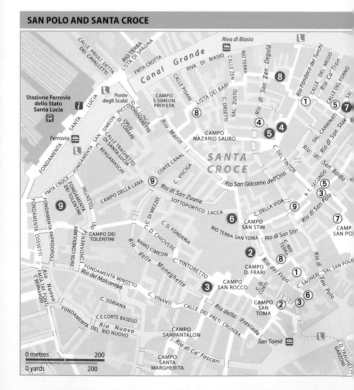

1 The Rialto
See pp34–5.

2 Santa Maria Gloriosa dei Frari

Known by all simply as the Frari (a corruption of *Frati*, meaning "friars"), this huge, plain Gothic church *(see pp32–3)* dwarfs the eastern section of San Polo. The first church was built by Fransiscan friars during 1250–1338, but was replaced by a larger building, which was completed by the mid-15th century. The interior is striking for its sheer size and for the quality of its works of art. These include masterpieces by Titan and Giovanni Bellini, as well as Donatello's famous John the Baptist and a number of imposing monuments to famous Venetians. The campanile, set into the left transept of the church, is the second largest in the city.

Scuola Grande di San Rocco

3 Scuola Grande di San Rocco

MAP K4 ▪ Campo S Rocco, S Polo 3052 ▪ Open 9:30am–5:30pm daily ▪ Closed 1 Jan, 25 Dec ▪ Adm ▪ www.scuolagrandesanrocco.it

Blinding in the morning sun, the early Renaissance façade of this historic building, home to master-pieces by Tintoretto, is a marvel of intertwined sculpted stone wreaths and crouching elephants dwarfed by stately columns. The Istrian stone facing is embedded with a medley of burgundy porphyry and green-and cream-veined marble inserts. Designed by Bartolomeo Bon in 1517 and added to by Scarpagnino among others, the imposing building with neighbouring church was home to one of the city's foremost confraternities, established in 1478, and honoured with an annual visit by the doge.

4 Campo San Giacomo dell'Orio

MAP L2

This quintessential picturesque square, well off the beaten track, sports plane trees, benches for relaxing and patches of grass. Modest surrounding palaces are home to Venice University's archi-tectural faculties. The laid-back air and abundance of eateries and coffee shops make it very inviting, and there's no lack of subjects for photographers or artists.

	Top 10 Sights
①	*see pp89–91*
①	**Places to Eat** *see p93*
①	**Craft Shops** *see p92*

5 Chiesa di San Giacomo dall'Orio

MAP L2 ■ Campo S Giacomo dell'Orio, S Croce ■ 041 275 04 62 ■ Open 10:30am–4:30pm Mon–Sat ■ Adm ■ www.chorusvenezia.org

Do not miss this unusual church. Founded in the 9th century, its Latin-cross shape boasts a marvellous 15th-century wood-beamed ceiling and a forest of colourful granite and black limestone columns from the Middle East, several of them loot from the Crusades. The floor merits close scrutiny for its multitude of fossils, while memorable paintings include Palma il Giovane's *Descent of Manna* (1580–81), left of the main altar, and a painted crucifix (1350) attributed to Paolo Veneziano.

6 Scuola Grande di San Giovanni Evangelista

MAP L3 ■ Campiello della Scuola, S Polo 2454 ■ 041 71 82 34 ■ Open daily (times vary) ■ Adm ■ www.scuolasangiovanni.it

This erstwhile confraternity head-quarters with a high-ceilinged upstairs hall is mostly used for conferences. The monumental staircase was the work of Coducci and the priceless reliquary contains a fragment of the True Cross, presented to the Scuola in 1369. The spectacular *Miracles of the Cross* cycle of paintings commissioned of Gentile Bellini and associates is now in the Accademia Galleries (*see pp30–31*). The exterior court-yard has a fine sculptured portal screen completed in 1485 by Pietro Lombardo mounted with an eagle to symbolize St John.

Scuola Grande di San Giovanni Evangelista

Palazzo Mocenigo

7 Palazzo Mocenigo

MAP M2 ■ Salizzada S Stae, S Croce 1992 ■ 041 72 17 98 ■ Open Apr–Oct: 10am–5pm Tue–Sun (to 4pm Nov–Mar); last admission 30 min before closing time ■ Closed 1 Jan, 1 May, 25 Dec ■ Adm ■ www.visitmuve.it

The richly furnished and frescoed rooms of this 18th-century patrician palace have showcases of historic fabrics and costumes, plus a fasci-nating history of perfumes. The Mocenigo family portrait gallery has a total of seven doges, topped in fame by Alvise I, the victor at the 1571 Battle of Lepanto against the Turks, which was crucial for the Republic.

8 Campo San Zan Degolà

MAP L1 ■ Chiesa di San Giovanni Decollato: open 10am–noon Mon–Sat

People usually hurry through this square en route to the bus terminal, oblivious to its quiet charm. Interest starts with the curious loggia on the western canal edge, then there's the attractive plain church named for San Giovanni Decollato or St John the Beheaded, depicted with flowing curly locks in a stone bas-relief on the southern wall. Inside the simple Veneto-Byzantine building are lovely 13th-century frescoes, an unusual survivor for damp old Venice.

⑨ Giardino Papadopoli
MAP J3

A leafy haven of twittering sparrows and flowerbeds close to Piazzale Roma and the car parks, these French-designed gardens date back to the 1800s when extravagant parties for the nobility were held here among exotic flowers and rare animals. Site of a demolished convent, it belonged to Corfu-born entrepreneurs, hence the Greek name. The public park was greatly reduced in size when the Rio Nuovo canal was excavated in 1932–3.

Giardino Papadopoli

⑩ Ca' Pesaro Museo di Arte Orientale
MAP N1 ■ Fondamenta Ca'Pesaro, S Croce 2076 ■ Open Apr–Oct: 10am–6pm Tue–Sun (to 5pm Nov–Mar); last admission 60 min before closing time ■ Adm ■ www.visitmuve.it

This impressive Oriental Art Collection is an eclectic mix of 19th-century curiosities from all over the Far East. Exhibits include armour, porcelain and costumes, lacquerwork boxes and musical instruments. The museum is on the third floor, above the modern art gallery in Ca' Pesaro (see p24). A single ticket grants admission into the gallery and the museum.

A DAY IN SAN POLO

▶ MORNING

Drink your fill of Tintoretto's dynamic paintings at the **Scuola Grande di San Rocco** (see p89) before wandering east to Campo San Polo. Coffee is a must in the square, either at one of the local bars or at the attractive **Antica Birraria La Corte** (see p93).

It's not far from here to **Rialto Market** (see pp34–5) for late-morning bargains of fresh produce, often nearing half-price when stall-holders are in a hurry to shut up shop. If this has worked up an appetite, a Grand Canal-side lunch is worth consideration at this point. There is a string of eateries spread along the sun-blessed **Riva del Vin**, close to the foot of Rialto Bridge. Each displays live lobster and fish and has multilingual menus. In winter diners sit in see-through "tents" so that views of the canal and the procession of boats are ensured.

AFTERNOON

Head north and explore the craft and gift shops, lace, scarf and T-shirt stalls along Ruga Rialto and the old red-light area of **Rio Terrà Rampani** (see p60).

Try to end up in pretty **Campo San Giacomo dell'Orio** (see p89) for a pre-dinner drink at **Al Prosecco** wine bar (Campo S Giacomo dell'Orio, S Croce 1503; 041 524 02 22; closed Sun). Ask for a delicious glass of the fruity red Refosco from Friuli and bocconcino con mortadella di cinghiale (bite-sized roll with sliced wild boar).

See map on pp88–9

Craft Shops

1 Gilberto Penzo
MAP M3 ■ Calle Seconda dei Saoneri, S Polo 2681

A visit to this workshop with beautiful wooden models of traditional Venetian boats is a real treat. Many crafts come in DIY kit form.

2 Mazzon le Borse
MAP L4 ■ Campiello S Tomà, S Polo 2807

Papà Piero has been making beautiful leather bags that last a lifetime since 1963. His family helps him in the workshop.

Hand-painting masks at Tragicomica

3 Tragicomica
MAP M4 ■ Calle dei Nomboli, S Polo 2800

The result of 20 years of creating elaborate papier-mâché and leather masks and brocade costumes for Carnival, as well as theatrical pro-ductions, can be appreciated in this spectacular craft shop, where staff explain the significance of pieces.

4 Rivoaltus
MAP P3 ■ Ponte di Rialto, S Polo 11

Beautiful hand-bound diaries and address books can be purchased from this tiny shop, which is situated right on the Rialto bridge.

5 Laberintho
MAP M2 ■ Calle del Scaleter, S Polo 2236

Two goldsmiths create contemporary jewellery pieces and replicas of antique rings. For a special souvenir, they will also make something tailored to your specifications.

6 Sabbie e Nebbie
MAP M4 ■ Calle dei Nomboli, S Polo 2768/A

Customers come to this boutique to purchase pottery, candles and other trinkets from Japan and Italy.

7 Attombri
MAP P2 ■ Sottoportego degli Orefici, S Polo 74

In an old covered passageway that has long been home to the Rialto Market goldsmiths, Attombri is run by two designer brothers who make limited-edition jewellery.

8 Dinamo
MAP L3 ■ Calle del Tagiapiera, S Polo 2599/A

A mix of ceramics, designer wares and fabrics created by local and foreign artisans are sold at Dinamo.

9 Margherita Rossetto Ceramica
MAP K2 ■ Corte Canal, S Croce 659

Eggcups, teapots and platters are some of the delightful hand-turned objects available here.

10 La Pedrera
MAP N2 ■ Calle Regina 2262, S Polo

Choose from handmade beads, photo frames and colourful Murano glass creations.

Necklaces at La Pedrera

Places to Eat

PRICE CATEGORIES

For a three-course meal for one with half a bottle of wine (or equivalent meal), taxes and extra charges.

€ under €40 €€ €40–60 €€€ over €60

Elegant dining area at Muro

1 La Zucca

MAP L1 ▪ Ponte del Megio, S Croce 1762 ▪ 041 524 15 70 ▪ Closed Sun ▪ €€

Delicious vegetarian fare is served here, and there is also the promise of unforgettable chocolate desserts.

2 Osteria Bancogiro

MAP P2 ▪ Campo S Giacometto, S Polo 122 ▪ 041 523 20 61 ▪ Closed Mon ▪ €€

This is a trendy restaurant-bar along the Grand Canal serving a variety of quality Italian vintages and tasty nibbles.

Osteria Bancogiro

3 Da Fiore

MAP M3 ▪ Calle del Scaleter, S Polo 2202/A ▪ 041 721 308 ▪ Closed Sun & Mon, 3 weeks in Jan, Aug ▪ €€€

The exclusive Da Fiore is possibly one of Venice's best restaurants. For great views, reserve the outdoor table on the balcony. Book in advance.

4 Il Refolo

MAP L2 ▪ Campo San Giacomo dell'Orio, S Croce 1459 ▪ 041 524 00 16 ▪ Closed Mon, Tue lunch ▪ €

Diners come to this great canal-side spot for inexpensive pizzas in a magical surrounding.

5 Osteria Mocenigo

MAP M1 ▪ Salizzada San Stae, S Croce 1919 ▪ 041 523 17 03 ▪ Closed Mon ▪ €

Don't miss the *cestino al parmiggiano*, a crisp fried pastry and cheese basket filled with prawns.

6 Muro

MAP N2 ▪ Campiello dello Spezier, S Croce 2048 ▪ 041 524 16 28 ▪ €

Order steak or fish here – Antipasto Muro is a great seafood selection.

7 Antica Birraria La Corte

MAP M3 ▪ Campo S Polo, S Polo 2168 ▪ 041 275 05 70 ▪ €

Pizzas named after the city's bridges are served at this ultra-modern eatery set in a former brewery. There is also a tree-shaded patio.

8 Gelateria Alaska

MAP K2 ▪ Calle Larga dei Bari, S Croce 1159 ▪ €

Unforgettable ice cream is made by a true maestro, Carlo the owner. This is the real deal – 100 per cent natural gelato with ginger, spearmint, rose petals, pistachio or green tea.

9 Taverna Da Baffo

MAP L3 ▪ Campiello Sant'Agostin, S Polo 2346 ▪ 041 524 20 61 ▪ €

Seek out this tranquil square for a light lunch with a glass of Belgian beer or crisp Friuli wine.

10 Pasticceria Rizzardini

MAP M3 ▪ Campiello dei Meloni, S Polo 1415 ▪ Closed Tue, Aug ▪ €

This old-style pastry shop serves thick hot chocolate and divine fruit tarts, almond slices and peanut toffee.

See map on pp88–9

TOP 10 Dorsoduro

Chiesa dei Gesuati, Zattere

A district of contrasts, Dorsoduro stretches from the port, via the panoramic Zattere and Grand Canal, all the way to the Punta della Dogana. Highlights for visitors include two foremost art galleries, the Accademia and the Peggy Guggenheim Collection *(see pp40–41)*, crammed with master-pieces ancient and modern, as well as Ca' Rezzonico palace *(see p46)* and magnificent churches, Santa Maria

della Salute *(see p48)* and San Sebastiano, the latter famous for its wonderful Veronese works. Literally the "hard backbone" of Venice, built on elevated islands of compacted subsoil, Dorsoduro used to be sparsely populated. Today, as home to most of the city's university premises, it is full of lively cafés, bars and nightlife, concentrated in the market square, Campo Santa Margherita.

DORSODURO

1 Top 10 Sights
see pp97–9

1 Places to Eat
see p101

1 Shops
see p100

Previous pages Basilica di Santa Maria della Salute, from the Campanile di San Marco

1 Accademia Galleries
See pp30–31.

2 Zattere
MAP C5

This broad waterfront took its name from the rafts of timber *(zattere)* floated downstream from the extensive forests in the northern Dolomite region which were managed by the Venetian Republic. The precious wood was either used for constructing palaces or transformed into masts and the like for the important shipbuilding industry. The tall-masted sailing ships and rowing boats that used to moor here have long since been replaced by motorized *vaporetti* and tourist launches, and nowadays the Zattere signifies lovely lagoon views and is perfect for a daytime or evening stroll.

3 San Nicolò dei Mendicoli
MAP A5 ■ Campo S Nicolò, Dorsoduro 1907 ■ 041 275 03 82 ■ Open 10am–noon, 3–5:30pm Mon–Sat, 9am–noon Sun

This Veneto-Byzantine church with an imposing square *campanile* (bell tower) is known to film buffs from Nicholas Roeg's chilling 1973 film *Don't Look Now*.

Hidden in a maze of alleyways off the port zone, it has a pretty portico that doubled as a shelter for the poor. Founded in the 7th century, it is the second-oldest church in Venice. In the 1970s it was restored by the Venice in Peril Fund, who waterproofed the low floor.

San Nicolò dei Mendicoli

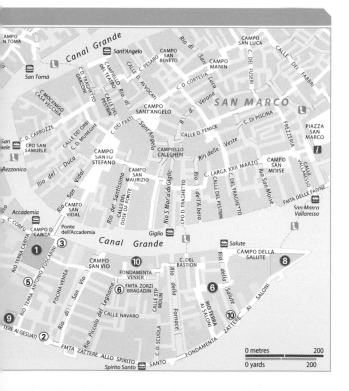

MASKS

Handmade in papier-mâché and glittery plaster, Venetian masks (right) are now strictly tourist fare, but they were once essential attire during Carnival, allowing aristocrats to enjoy themselves in anonymity. One unusual model, with a long curved nose, was used by doctors during plagues, its cavity filled with perfumed herbs to filter the diseased air.

4 Squero di San Trovaso

MAP C5

This is the city's most famous gondola repair and construction yard, though its days may be numbered. The combined workshop-dwelling is reminiscent of an Alpine chalet, as the first occupants came from the mountainous Cadore region. Closed to visitors, it backs on to a canal (Rio di San Trovaso), so it's easy to watch the caulking and cleaning in progress.

5 Chiesa di San Sebastiano

MAP B5 ■ Campo S Sebastiano, Dorsoduro 1907 ■ 041 275 04 62 ■ Open 10:30am–4:30pm Mon–Sat ■ Adm ■ www.chorusvenezia.org

This 16th-century church (see p49) is a treasure trove of Paolo Veronese paintings. The artist devoted most of his life to its fresco cycle.

6 Rio Terrà dei Catecumeni

MAP D5

A reclaimed thoroughfare between the Zattere and Santa Maria della Salute, this stretch is dominated by a long building, a school, where prisoners-of-war of the Republic who did not profess the Christian faith were held captive until they converted. This quiet backwater comes alive on 21 November with the Salute festivities (see p77).

7 Campo Santa Margherita

The sprawling square of Santa Margherita (see pp38–9), lined with houses from the 14th and 15th centuries, is the lively hub of western Dorsoduro. Market stalls, offbeat shops and cafés attract many young people. The colourful fish stalls sell live eels and lobster, the *erborista* alternative medicine, and the bakers some of the tastiest loaves in Venice. The former church of Santa Margherita, now an auditorium owned by the university, lies to the north of the square. Visitors can see sculptural fragments from the original 18th-century church, including gargoyles on the truncated campanile and adjacent house.

8 Punta della Dogana

MAP E5 ■ Campo della Salute, Dorsoduro 2 ■ 041 523 16 80 ■ 10am–7pm Wed–Mon ■ Adm ■ www.palazzograssi.it

This exciting addition to the Venetian contemporary art scene is housed in an imposing 17th-century customs building, the interior of which was renovated by Japanese architect Tadao Ando. It contains important works, including pieces by British artists Rachel Whiteread and the Chapman Brothers, and offers fantastic views towards St Mark's, San Giorgio and the two main canals of Venice. Tickets also grant entry into the Palazzo Grassi (see p82).

Punta della Dogana

Altar in Chiesa dei Gesuati

9 Chiesa dei Gesuati
MAP C5 ▪ Fondamente delle
Zattere, Dorsoduro 917 ▪ 041 275 06
42 ▪ Open 10:30am–4:30pm Mon–Sat
▪ Adm ▪ www.chorus venezia.org

Set right on the Zattere waterfront
close to the main ferry moorings, the
Gesuati (also known as Santa Maria
del Rosario) is often confused with
the Gesuiti (Jesuit) establishment
in Cannaregio. Taking over from a
minor religious order, the Domenican
friars had this church constructed
in Classical style in 1726 by Giorgio
Massari. Inside, the ceiling consists
of three uplifting frescoes (1737–9) by
Tiepolo (see p54), considered among
his best work, portraying St Dominic
amid glorious angels in flight.

10 Peggy Guggenheim Collection
Intended as a four-storey palace,
this building never rose beyond the
ground floor. It was in 1949, that
the building was bought as a home
by Peggy Guggenheim, a collector,
dealer and patron of the arts. She
had her vast collection of modern
European and American art in this
museum (see pp40–1), which
was inaugurated in 1980. Today,
Guggenheim remains Venice's
most visited sights. The light-filled
rooms and the modern canvases
provide a striking contrast to the
Renaissance paintings which are
the main attraction in Venetian
churches and museums.

EXPLORING DORSODURO

▶ **MORNING**

The **Accademia Galleries** (see
pp30–31) can be overwhelming,
so focus your visit on a selection
of its masterpieces, but don't
neglect the Carpaccios and
Bellinis. After all that art, have
a relaxing coffee watching the
boats go by at **Snack Bar
Accademia Foscarini** (Rio Terrà
Antonio Foscarini, Dorsoduro
878/C; 041 522 72 81; closed Tue),
a magical spot right at the foot
of Accademia Bridge.

Next, head off east for a leisurely
stroll, past Longhena's work of
art, the church of **Santa Maria
della Salute** (see p48), to **Punta
della Dogana**, a great spot for
taking photos of Piazza San
Marco. Turn back in the direction
of the **Zattere** and Giudecca
Canal. Lunch is recommended
at **Al Chioschetto** (Zattere,
Dorsoduro 1406/A), a bar right
on the water's edge.

AFTERNOON

Wander through to **Campo
Santa Margherita** to the
Scuola Grande dei Carmini
to admire Tiepolo's canvases,
then take time to admire the
architectural curiosities of
this fascinating square.

As sunset approaches waste no
time in occupying a table for a
Spritz aperitivo at the trendy bar
Margaret DuChamp (Campo S
Margherita, Dorsoduro 3019; 041
528 62 55; closed Tue). It's hard to
better this as a place for people-
watching, and an added bonus
is the scent of jasmine that fills
the air as night falls.

See map on pp96–7 ←

Shops

1 3856
MAP K4 ■ Calle San Pantalon, Dorsoduro 3749

A small but perfectly assembled selection of clothing and accessories is available at this shop run by a friendly mother-and-daughter team.

2 Bottega Tramontin Gondole
MAP K5 ■ Calle del Fabbro, Dorsoduro 3282

This shop sells lovely handmade ornaments, souvenirs and jewellery inspired by traditional Venetian gondolas. Many of the items have been crafted using wood from real gondolas.

3 Totem-Il Canale Gallery
MAP C5 ■ Rio Terrà Antonio Foscarini, Dorsoduro 878/B

Bulky ancient beads, made with vitreous paste and once traded in Africa, count as precious antiques. There are modern African wood artworks too.

4 Signor Blum
MAP K5 ■ Campo S Barnaba, Dorsoduro 2840

Detailed jigsaw models of Gothic palaces, flanked by wall panels and painted toy figures are handmade by this co-operative of female artisans.

Signor Blum

5 Augusto Mazzon
MAP L5 ■ Calle del Traghetto, Dorsoduro 2783

Everyone's Christmas tree needs one of the joyous gilded cherubs lovingly crafted by wood-carver and painter Danilo. He also makes picture frames and furniture.

6 Officina Veneziana
MAP K4 ■ Campo S Pantalon, Dorsoduro 3701

Choose from a wonderful selection of Art Deco jewellery, Easter eggs, Christmas decorations and fine china.

7 Perla Madre Design
MAP K5 ■ Calle delle Botteghe, Dorsoduro 3182

Colourful glass bead jewellery is made right in front of your eyes by designer Simona Iacovazzi.

Trendy design shop Madera

8 Madera
MAP K5 ■ Campo S Barnaba, Dorsoduro 2762

This contemporary design store has minimalist pieces in wood and glass, as well as gorgeous ceramics.

9 Libreria Toletta
MAP L6 ■ Sacca della Toletta, Dorsoduro 1213

Specializing in art and architecture, this popular bookshop also has a great collection of guidebooks and novels in English.

10 Arras
MAP L5 ■ Campiello Squelini, Dorsoduro 3235

This shop stocks original hand-woven fabrics, garments and bags in beautiful colours.

Places to Eat

PRICE CATEGORIES
For a three-course meal for one with half
a bottle of wine (or equivalent meal),
taxes and extra charges.

€ under €40 €€ €40–60 €€€ over €60

1 Gelateria Nico
MAP C5 ■ Zattere,
Dorsoduro 922 ■ 041 522
52 93 ■ Closed Thu ■ €

This spot is Venice's
most renowned ice-
cream parlour. *Gianduiotto
da passeggio* – hazelnut
and chocolate ice cream
smothered in whipped
cream – is a local favourite.

*Gianduiotto da
passeggio*

2 Ristorante La Calcina
MAP C5 ■ Zattere, Dorsoduro
780 ■ 041 520 64 66 ■ €€

Mediterranean and Venetian cuisine,
including a wide range of vegetarian
dishes, are served at this restaurant
with a lovely canalside terrace.

3 La Bitta
MAP K6 ■ Calle Lunga de San
Barnaba, Dorsoduro 2753 ■ 041 523
05 31 ■ No credit cards ■ Closed Sun
■ €€

Fine Italian wines accompany
a superb menu at this no-fish
restaurant *(see p69)*. Leave room
for one of their delicious desserts.

4 Impronta Caffè
MAP K4 ■ Calle dei Preti,
Dorsoduro 3815 ■ 041 275 03 86
■ Closed Sun ■ €

Affordable meals and long opening
hours make this a local favourite.

5 La Rivista
MAP C5 ■ Rio Terrà Foscarini,
Dorsoduro 979/A ■ 041 240 14 25
■ Closed Mon ■ €€

Innovative Italian cuisine is offered
here, in relaxing, designer modern
surroundings. There is an inspiring
choice of cold platters of cheese and
meats. The wine list is impressive.

6 Ai Gondolieri
MAP D5 ■ Ponte del Formager,
Dorsoduro 366 ■ 041 528 63 96
■ Closed Tue ■ €€

One of the city's top restaurants, Ai
Gondolieri specializes in game from
the Veneto when in season.

7 Suzie Café
MAP B5 ■ Campo S
Basilio, Dorsoduro 1527 ■ €

This great bar, frequented
by students, serves sand-
wiches, pasta and salads.

8 Pasticceria Tonolo
MAP K4 ■ Crosera
S Pantalon, Dorsoduro 3764
■ 041 523 72 09 ■ Closed Mon ■ €

Delicious, freshly baked almond
biscuits and mini pizzas are just some
of the treats at Pasticceria Tonolo,
one of the city's best pastry shops.

9 Gelateria Il Doge
MAP K5 ■ Campo S Margherita,
Dorsoduro 3058A ■ 041 523 46 07
■ Closed Dec & Jan ■ €

Treat yourself to the *zuppa del doge*
(candied fruit, egg custard and
sponge cake soaked in Marsala)
at this great ice-cream parlour.

10 Linea d'Ombra
MAP D5 ■ Ponte dell'Umiltà,
Dorsoduro 19 ■ 041 241 18 81
■ Closed Tue, Dec–Feb ■ €€€

Enjoy the waterside setting behind
the landmark Salute church. Specialities on the menu include tuna
tartare and sea bass in a salt crust.

Linea d'Ombra

See map on pp96–7

TOP10 Cannaregio

Accounting for the huge crescent between the northern bank of the Grand Canal and the lagoon, the bustling *sestiere* of Cannaregio reaches from the railway station to the city hospital. It was home to Marco Polo and artists Titian and Tintoretto, and boasts landmark churches such as Madonna dell'Orto *(see p49)* along with the old Jewish Ghetto. Named after the *canne* (reeds) that once filled its marshes, it is crossed by Strada Nova, the city's main thoroughfare, but also contains Venice's narrowest alley, the 58-cm- (23-inch-) wide Calle Varisco. This vibrant area has its own market, craft workshops and rowing clubs, while relaxation comes at the string of shady parks and laid-back cafés and bars that line the maze of backstreet canals.

Campo dei Mori

CANNAREGIO

① Ca' d'Oro

MAP N1 ■ Calle Ca' d'Oro, Cannaregio 3932 ■ 041 520 03 45 ■ Open 8:15am–2pm Mon, 8:15am–7:15pm Tue–Sat, 9am–7pm Sun ■ Adm ■ www.cadoro.org

Behind the resplendent palace's *(see p46)* beautiful Gothic tracery is a column-filled courtyard paved with coloured tesserae. Inside is the Galleria Giorgio Franchetti, a collection of paintings, sculptures and ceramics donated to the State by Baron Giorgio Franchetti in 1916, along with the building. One highlight is Andrea Mantegna's painting *St Sebastian* (1560) pierced by arrows "like a hedgehog", in the portico leading to a loggia overlooking the Grand Canal. An ornate 15th-century staircase leads to 16th-century Flemish tapestries on the second floor.

Jewish Ghetto, once a closed island

② Jewish Ghetto

MAP C1 ■ Museo Ebraico, Campo del Ghetto Nuovo, Cannaregio 2902/B ■ 041 715 359 ■ Open 10am–5:30pm Sun–Fri (to 7pm Jun–Sep) ■ Closed public and Jewish holidays ■ Adm

The word "ghetto" originated in Venice, derived from *getto* (casting) due to an old iron foundry here. As of 1492, many Jewish refugees reached Venice after expulsion from Spain and in 1516 they were obliged by law to move to this area. Subject to a curfew to prevent their fraternizing with local women, they slept behind locked gates, their island circled by an armed patrol boat. Waves of arrivals saw each language group build its own synagogue and raise the buildings to seven floors in height. Today around 30 Jews still live in the ghetto, while a further 470 reside in other parts of the city. The synagogues can be visited with a guide, and there's the Museo Ebraico (museum of sacred objects).

③ Corte Seconda del Milion

MAP Q2

The restructured Malibran Theatre, situated in this photogenic square, was erected in the 1790s on the site of a house, where the famous 13th-century explorer Marco Polo was born *(see p50)*. Other early Gothic buildings remain, their timber overhangs set off by bright-red geraniums. Along with the adjoining bridge, the square was named in honour of the explorer whose stories about the Orient in *Il Milione* continue to inspire travellers.

Santa Maria dei Miracoli

(4) Santa Maria dei Miracoli
MAP Q2 ▪ Campo dei Miracoli, Cannaregio ▪ 041 275 04 62 ▪ Open 10:30am–4:30pm Mon–Sat ▪ Adm ▪ www.chorus venezia.org

A "jewellery box" of marble slabs and exquisite bas-reliefs, this Renaissance church *(see p48)*was named after a miracle-working icon from 1409, said to have resuscitated a drowned man and now enshrined in the main altar.

(5) Campo dei Mori
MAP D1

In this odd, funnel-shaped square your attention is drawn to three statues of Arabian-style "Moors" – but neither North African nor Muslim, they hailed from Morea in Greece. Rioba, Sandi and Afani Mastelli were medieval traders who made their home in the family palace around the corner. Next to the bridge over Rio della Sensa is a doorway marked No. 3399, once the home of renowned 16th-century artist Tintoretto *(see p54).*

(6) Farmacia Ponci
MAP D2 ▪ Strada Nova, Cannaregio 2233/A

The "Casa degli Speziali", the oldest pharmacy in Venice, carries on its

---

business in modern premises alongside its restored 16th-century rooms. Displayed on original briar-wood shelving adorned with Baroque statues in Arolla pinewood are rows of 17th-century porcelain jars used for storing medicinal ingredients; for safety reasons, poisons were kept in a rear room. Pharmacies in Venice were strictly regulated and numbered 518 in 1564, the year their guild was formed.

(7) Fondamente della Misericordia and degli Ormesini
MAP C2

Parallel to the Strada Nova but worlds away from the tourist bustle, these adjoining quaysides have a real neighbourhood feel. There's a good sprinkling of *osterie* (wine bars) alongside Mexican and Middle Eastern restaurants, a continuation of former trade links: the word *"ormesini"* derives from a rich fabric traded through Hormuz, now in Iran, and imitated in Florence and Venice. Ormesini leads into Misericordia and to the towering red-brick Scuola Grande building. Used as the city's basketball team headquarters for many years, it occasionally opens for temporary exhibitions.

Fondamente della Misericordia

(8) Palazzo Labia
MAP C2 ▪ Campo S Geremia, Cannaregio ▪ Closed to the public

Abandoned when its wealthy merchant owners fled to Vienna at the fall of the Republic, this 17th-century palace overlooking the Canal di Cannaregio acted as a silk factory, saw-mill and

---

THE JEWS IN VENICE

Banned by Republic law from practising manual trades, many Jews were skilled doctors or moneylenders. Most were refugees from other parts of Europe, and they are credited with introducing rice-based dishes to Venetian cuisine. As remembered by a memorial in the ghetto, few returned from the Nazi camps of World War II.

primary school, but was badly damaged in 1945 when a boat loaded with munitions blew up in front of it. Luckily, the wonderful ballroom frescoed by Tiepolo has been restored. The palace belongs to RAI, the state broadcasting service.

Ceiling fresco of Chiesa di Sant'Alvise

9 Chiesa di Sant'Alvise
MAP C1 ■ Campo S Alvise, Cannaregio ■ Open 10:30am–4pm Mon–Fri, 10:30am–4:30pm Sat & Sun ■ Adm ■ www.chorusvenezia.org

This church is said to have been commissioned by a Venetian noblewoman in 1388 to honour Saint Louis of Toulouse after the saint appeared to her in a dream. Major restoration took place in the 17th century, when the ceiling was painted with frescoes by Pietro Antonio Torri and Pietro Ricchi. Other notable works of art in the church include paintings by Giambattista Tiepolo – *Ascent to Calvary*, *Crowning with Thorns* and *The Flagellation*.

10 Fondamente Nuove
MAP E2

Opposite the cemetery island of San Michele *(see p118)*, this lagoon-side pavement is an important jumping-off point for ferries to the northern islands and sports one of the city's rare petrol stations. The ample quaysides were not constructed and paved until the mid-1500s; until then the waterfront reached back to Titian's garden (No. 5113, Calle Larga dei Botteri), giving unobstructed views of the Alps on a clear day.

EXPLORING CANNAREGIO

Fondamenta della Sacca · Madonna dell'Orto · Al Timon · Ponte dei Tre Archi · Campo dei Mori · Bottega del Caffè · Jewish Ghetto · Hostaria alla Fontana · Strada Nova · Ca d'Oro

▶ MORNING

Begin the day with the Galleria Franchetti in the lovely **Ca d'Oro** *(see p103)*, but leave plenty of time for the balconies that overlook the Grand Canal and the mosaics in the courtyard. Afterwards, follow **Strada Nova** in the direction of the railway station to the **Bottega del Caffè** *(Calle del Pistor, Cannaregio 1903; 041 714 232; closed Wed)* for the best coffee in Cannaregio. Only minutes away is the fascinating **Jewish Ghetto** *(see p103)*, where you can take an informative guided tour of the many remaining synagogues in the area.

For a revitalizing break, lunch at **Hostaria alla Fontana** is recommended *(Fondamenta di Cannaregio, Cannaregio 1102; 041 715 077; closed Apr–Oct: Tue; Nov–Mar: Sun)*.

AFTERNOON

Wander up the canal towards the unusual, three-arched **Ponte dei Tre Archi** *(see p58)*. Return over the bridge and head for **Fondamenta della Sacca**, which affords good views of the Dolomites on a clear day. Many ways lead east from here, but try to take in the church of **Madonna dell'Orto** *(see p49)* for the Tintoretto paintings, then **Campo dei Mori** to see the house where the artist once lived.

On Fondamenta Ormesini, pop into **Al Timon**, where energetic waiters will serve you a glass of north Italian wine *(Fondamenta Ormesini, Cannaregio 2754; 041 524 60 66; closed Wed)*.

See map on pp102–3 ←

Specialist Shops

1 Tà Kalà

MAP D2 ■ Strada Nova, Cannaregio 4391/C

Close to Campo SS Apostoli, this gift shop is a stockist of fascinating holograms, Murano glass delights, masks and chunky jewellery.

2 Mori & Bozzi
MAP D2 ■ Rio Terrà della Maddalena, Cannaregio 2367

One of the best shoe shops in Venice offers an irresistible selection of women's footwear, clothes and accessories.

3 San Leonardo Market
MAP C2 ■ Rio Terrà San Leonardo ■ Mon–Sat

In the morning and late afternoon this area functions as a lively open-air produce market. In autumn the air is thick with the aroma of roasting chestnuts.

San Leonardo Market

4 Lili e Paolo Darin
MAP C2 ■ Salizzada S Geremia, Cannaregio 317

Come here for original handmade glass beads in brilliant hues and myriad shapes, window hangings and Christmas decorations.

5 Costumi Nicolao Atelier
MAP C1 ■ Fondamenta dei Ormesini, Cannaregio 2590

This is the place to go to hire a Carnival outfit. It offers a wide range of period costumes and formal evening wear. It also organizes mask-making courses.

Paintings for sale at Codex

6 Codex
MAP C2 ■ Fondamenta Ormesini, Cannaregio 2778

This studio and exhibition space of resident artists Nelson Kishi and Robin Frood sells original drawings, paintings, prints and posters.

7 Miani
MAP Q2 ■ Salizzada S Canciano, Canareggio 5577

Handmade Murano glass beads are turned into beautiful jewellery by the family that runs this shop. Demonstrations of the crafting process are held on the premises.

8 Salmoiraghi & Viganò
MAP D2 ■ Strada Nova, Cannaregio 3928–3930

Italian spectacles are stylish and good value, and this well-reputed optometrist can make up prescription glasses the same day.

9 Marco Polo Bookshop
MAP Q2 ■ Calle del Teatro Malibran, Cannaregio 5886/A

This friendly, well-stocked store carries English-language volumes on Venice, as well as offering a book-exchange programme.

10 Gianni Basso
MAP E2 ■ Calle del Fumo, Cannaregio 5306

The marvellous handmade stationery on offer at this shop is made by a modest artisan and is popular with international VIPs.

Places to Eat

 Ristorante Al Fontego dei Pescatori
MAP D2 ■ Calle Priuli, Cannaregio 3726 ■ 041 520 05 38 ■ €

This classy seafood restaurant with a lovely courtyard for summer dining is noted for its seasonal specialities.

Canal-side dining tables at Da Rioba

Il Gelatone
MAP D2 ■ Rio Terrà della Maddalena, Cannaregio 2063 ■ €

Try the creamy and delicious *bacio* (kiss) of hazelnut and chocolate at this ice cream shop.

Ostaria Boccadoro
MAP E3 ■ Campo Widman, Cannaregio 5405 ■ 041 521 10 21 ■ €€€

Pasta dishes and delicate blends of seafood and seasonal vegetables are on offer here *(see p68)*, as well as desserts and an extensive wine list.

Taverna del Campiello Remer
MAP D3 ■ Campiello Remer, Cannaregio 5701 ■ 041 522 87 89 ■ Closed Wed ■ €€€

This converted warehouse has upturned barrels as tables and offers a delicious buffet menu.

Il Santo Bevitore
MAP D2 ■ Campo S Fosca, Cannaregio 2393 ■ Closed Sun ■ €

Enjoy a drink and snack at this laid-back bar with live music. There is a good range of quality beers.

Vini da Gigio
MAP D2 ■ Fondamenta S Felice, Cannaregio 3628/A ■ 041 528 51 40 ■ Closed Mon & Tue, 2 weeks in Aug ■ €€

Canal-side restaurant *(see p68)* serving innovative traditional dishes.

Al Parlamento
MAP B2 ■ Fondamenta Savorgnan, Cannaregio 511 ■ 041 244 02 14 ■ €

Appetizing, simple meals are served at this canal-side café.

Da Rioba
MAP C1 ■ Fondamenta della Misericordia, Cannaregio 2553 ■ 041 524 43 79 ■ Closed Mon ■ €€–€€€

The impeccably presented Venetian fish-based dishes on the menu at this restaurant are given a tasteful modern twist.

Osteria Anice Stellato
MAP C1 ■ Fondamenta della Sensa, Cannaregio 3272 ■ 041 720 744 ■ Closed Mon & Tue, 2 weeks in Aug ■ €€

It is important to book well ahead for this popular place. Among the culinary delights on offer are fish and meat dishes, as well as a wonderful *zabaglione* dessert.

La Bottega Ai Promessi Sposi
MAP P1 ■ Calle dell'Oca, Cannaregio 4367 ■ 041 241 27 47 ■ Closed Mon & Wed lunch ■ €

This low-key restaurant offers diners tasty *cicchetti* (bar snacks) while friendly staff serve more substantial traditional Venetian fare.

See map on pp102–3

TOP 10 Castello

Named after a castle possibly built here in Roman times, Castello is the "fishtail" of Venice. The western half of the district is crammed with historic highlights such as the churches of SS Giovanni e Paolo and San Zaccaria *(see p48)*. However, half of Castello is taken up with shipbuilding, focusing on the historic Arsenale. The tree-lined Giardini is the venue for the Biennale *(see p111)*.

Riva degli Schiavoni

CASTELLO

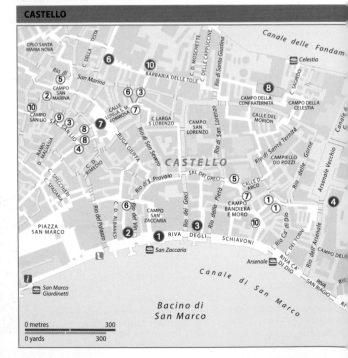

1 Riva degli Schiavoni
MAP F4

Thronging with tour groups and packed with souvenir stalls, this quayside affords a lovely promenade past majestic palaces (now mostly hotels) and a much photographed 1887 monument to the first king of Italy, Vittorio Emanuele. It is linked to Piazza San Marco by the elegant Istrian stone bridge Ponte della Paglia, named after the *paglia* (straw) once unloaded from barges here. This is also the best place for taking pictures of the Bridge of Sighs. At the eastern end is the Ca' di Dio ("house of God"), a 13th-century hospice for pilgrims en route to the Holy Land.

2 Hotel Danieli

This enchanting 15th-century palace with a pink Gothic façade is set on the magnificent waterfront near Piazza San Marco. After a string of aristocratic proprietors, it was taken over in 1822 by Joseph da Niel, who turned it into a hotel with an illustrious guest list, including Dickens, Wagner and Ruskin. In the 1940s an annexe was added amid great controversy – since 1102 no dwelling over one floor had been allowed on the site. The redeeming feature of the 1940s wing is the roof restaurant (see p146).

Eye-catching front of Hotel Danieli

3 Santa Maria della Pietà
MAP F4 ■ Riva degli Schiavoni, Castello 3700 ■ Open 10am–6pm Tue–Sun ■ Adm ■ www.pietavenezia.org

Inextricably linked with the composer and musician Antonio Vivaldi, this Classical-fronted church designed by Giorgio Massari belonged to the adjoining home for foundlings where he taught. It is best seen by attending an evening concert to appreciate Tiepolo's uplifting ceiling fresco, exalting music and the young choristers, identifiable by the sprigs of pomegranate blossom they wear. The choir stalls accommodated both the singers and the nobility, who were not expected to mix with the commoners.

Santa Maria della Pietà

4 Arsenale
MAP G3 ▪ Castello

Aptly named after the Arab word *darsina'a* ("house of industry"), Venice's formidable Arsenale shipyards at their peak employed an army of 16,000 to produce the fleets that sailed the Mediterranean, spreading and protecting the influence of the Republic through trade deals and naval superiority. With its innovative assembly-line system, the Arsenale could construct a galley in a few hours, notably in 1574 while the French king Henry III enjoyed a banquet. The stone lions that guard the entrance hail from Greek islands looted by Venetian commanders.

Crenellated entrance to Arsenale

5 San Pietro di Castello
MAP H4 ▪ Chiesa di San Pietro di Castello ▪ Open 10:30am–4:30pm Mon, 10:30am–4:30pm Tue–Sat ▪ Adm ▪ www.chorusvenezia.org

It is hard to imagine that Venice's religious headquarters were here until 1807, when the Basilica di San Marco became the city's cathedral. Linked to the rest of Castello by two broad bridges, San Pietro attracts artists for its evocative, forlorn air, and fun-lovers for the late-June neighbourhood fair. Art lovers come for the church with work by Veronese and Coducci.

6 Campo Santi Giovanni e Paolo
MAP E3

Dominated by the brick façade of the Gothic church SS Giovanni e Paolo, this breezy square welcomes visitors with a flotilla of outdoor cafés. Worthy of contemplation is one of the world's most magnificent equestrian statues, a stylized 15th-century portrait of the great *condottiere* Bartolomeo Colleoni. He left a legacy to the city on the condition that his statue be erected in front of San Marco, craftily "interpreted" by the governors as the nearby Scuola Grande di San Marco. Gracefully decorated with arches and trompe l'oeil panels by Lombard masters, the former confraternity serves as the public hospital.

7 Campo Santa Maria Formosa
MAP E3 ▪ Chiesa di Santa Maria Formosa ▪ Open 10:30am–4:30pm Mon–Sat ▪ Adm ▪ www.chorus venezia.org

A lovely rounded church on this sun-blessed square appears to spread in all directions, the result of a 7th-century bishop's vision of the *formosa* ("shapely") Virgin Mary's request that it be built where "a white cloud came to rest". Artworks are by Vivarini and Palma il Vecchio. The square is a good place for a picnic or a game of football, in lieu of the bullfights and re-enactments of Venice's conquests held here in the olden days.

8 Chiesa di San Francesco della Vigna
MAP F3 ▪ Campo S Francesco della Vigna, Castello 2786 ▪ 041 520 61 02 ▪ Open 8am–12:30pm, 3–7pm Mon–Sat, 3–6:30pm Sun

In the back alleys of Castello, this Franciscan church sports a combination of architectural styles courtesy of both Sansovino and Palladio *(see p55)*, who designed the façade. The colonnaded cloister can be seen while you're admiring Giovanni Bellini's *Madonna and Child* (1507). Another highlight is Veronese's *Virgin and Child with Saints* (1551). Playgrounds have replaced the 13th-century *vigna* (vineyard).

Campo Santi Giovanni e Paolo

9 Via Garibaldi and Giardini

MAP H5

A pleasant avenue lined with cafés and a market, Via Garibaldi was named when the eponymous general marched into Venice in 1866 as part of his campaign for Unification. Take a stroll to the Giardini (public gardens). To make way for the park in 1807, architect Selva (see p55) demolished four churches and convents and a sailors' hospice.

Via Garibaldi

10 Ospedaletto

MAP F3 ■ Barbaria delle Tole, Castello 6691 ■ Open for pre-booked guided tours only (email: booking@fondazioneveneziaservizi.it) ■ Adm

The sculptures on the façade of this almshouse church, built in 1575, were added by Longhena in 1674. Pass through the church to the Sala della Musica, where female wards of the orphanage once gave concerts.

THE VENICE BIENNALE

The Giardini and its beautiful tree-lined avenues (below) were inaugurated as an international exhibition area in 1895 under the entrepreneur Count Volpi di Misurata. Every two years, more than 50 countries send artists to represent them, each with their own pavilion custom-designed by some of the world's leading architects, such as Alvar Aalto, Carlo Scarpa and James Stirling.

A DAY IN CASTELLO

Campo S. Giovanni e Paolo — Hospital
Scuola di San Giorgio degli Schiavoni
Campo Santa Maria Formosa
San Pietro di Castello
Campo San Zaccaria
Angiò Bar *Via Garibaldi*
Giuseppe Garibaldi Statue
Giardini

▶ MORNING

After a visit to the Gothic church on **Campo Santi Giovanni e Paolo**, wander through the city's **hospital**. Although it is now ultra-modern inside, you can still appreciate the wonderful Renaissance façade, and a series of ancient courtyards and confraternity buildings. Continue the historic theme with a coffee and cake at old-style Rosa Salva *(Campo SS Giovanni e Paolo, Castello 6779; 041 522 79 49)*.

Take a stroll, via **Campo Santa Maria Formosa**, to **Campo San Zaccaria** and the church with its Bellini painting, and **Scuola di San Giorgio degli Schiavoni** *(see p57)* for its Carpaccio works. For lunch, **Via Garibaldi** is a good bet, at one of the cafés or at Il Nuovo Galeon *(041 520 46 56; closed Tue)*.

AFTERNOON

Head east along **Via Garibaldi**, and detour briefly into the shady avenue for the statue of Giuseppe Garibaldi and his followers. After a visit to the island of **San Pietro di Castello**, make your way back via the lagoon and the **Giardini**. A poignant sculpture to the female partisans of World War II can be seen at water level.

Head in the direction of San Marco, just past the mouth of Via Garibaldi. On the embankment is **Angiò Bar**, the perfect spot for a Venetian sunset together with a glass of wine, not to mention all manner of delicious snacks *(Riva di S Biasio, Castello 2142; 041 277 85 55; closed Tue)*.

See map on pp108–9 ◀

Specialist Shops

1 Le Ceramiche
MAP F4 ■ Calle del Pestrin, Castello 3876

Alessandro Merlin crafts original plates, cups and tiles with black and white designs based on lagoon fish or human figures in this tiny atelier close to the Arsenale (see p110).

2 VizioVirtù Cioccolateria
MAP E3 ■ Calle Forneri, Castello 5988

This artisan chocolate factory creates mouthwatering chocolates from traditional Venetian recipes. Specialities include spiced hot chocolate and pralines. Book a guided tasting tour at info@viziovirtu.com.

3 Papier Mâché
MAP R3 ■ Calle Lunga Santa Maria Formosa, Castello 5174

One of the few authentic mask shops in town also sells beautiful ceramics.

4 Il Papiro
MAP E4 ■ Calle delle Bande, Castello 5275

You can find tempting gifts in the shape of marbled paper-covered boxes, greetings cards and writing paper with artistic letterheads here.

5 Bragorà
MAP F4 ■ Salita Sant'Antonin, Castello 3496

This shop has an eclectic mix of design, art and creative objects, many of them sourced from local designers.

Stylish Bragorà

Books stacked at Libreria Acqua Alta

6 Libreria Acqua Alta
MAP R3 ■ Calle Longa S Maria Formosa, Castello 5176

With ancient volumes piled high and Venetian-specific literature, this is a fascinating bookshop with a gondola full of books inside.

7 Muranero
MAP F4 ■ Salizzada del Pignater, Castello 3545

Senegalese artist Niang Moulaye creates beautiful handmade jewellery, combining ethnic African style with Murano glass bead-making techniques.

Venetian mask

8 Ratti
MAP F4 ■ Salizzada S Lio, Castello 5825

This eclectic shop sells household items such as the quintessential Italian coffee pot, along with mobile phones and hardware.

9 Corte delle Fate
MAP E3 ■ Salizzada S Lio, Castello 5690

Ultra-modern footwear and quirky accessories are available here in the shape of bags, jewellery and garments for the young.

10 Giovanna Zanella
MAP Q3 ■ Calle Carminati, Castello 5641

A must for all serious shoppers, this store offers quirky handmade shoes in a fabulous range of incredible designs.

Places to Eat

1 Corte Sconta
MAP F4 ■ Calle del Pestrin,
Castello 3886 ■ 041 522 70 24
■ Closed Sun & Mon, Jan, mid-Jul–
mid-Aug ■ €€€

One of Venice's finest restaurants,
Corte Sconta is known for its delicious
seafood antipasti. Book in advance.

2 Caffè La Serra
MAP H5 ■ Viale Giuseppe
Garibaldi, Castello 1254 ■ 041
296 03 60 ■ €

Housed in a former greenhouse, La
Serra is perfect for a light snack after
exploring the gardens of the Biennale.

3 Boutique del Gelato
MAP E3 ■ Salizzada S Lio,
Castello 5727 ■ 041 522 32 83
■ Closed Dec & Jan ■ €

There's inevitably a queue outside
this popular *gelateria*. Try the
tangy *limone* (lemon) or *fragola*
(strawberry) ice cream or creamy
gianduiotto (hazelnut-chocolate).

4 Trattoria dal Tosi Piccoli
MAP H5 ■ Secco Marina,
Castello 736–738 ■ 041 523 71 02
■ Closed Wed & Christmas ■ €

This cheery restaurant is especially
popular during the Biennale art
show (see p76). Mouthwatering *pasta
della casa* (house pasta) includes
seafood and vegetables. There is a
pizza menu at dinner.

5 Osteria di Santa Marina
MAP Q2 ■ Campo S Marina,
Castello 5911 ■ 041 528 52 39 ■ Closed
Sun, Mon lunch, 2 weeks in Jan ■ €€€

Sample creative versions of Venetian
and Italian fare at this well-reputed
restaurant. In summer, diners can
enjoy candlelight dining outside.

6 Alla Rivetta
MAP E4 ■ Ponte S Provolo,
Castello 4625 ■ 041 528 73 02
■ Closed Mon ■ €€

This friendly eatery has good seafood
options and regional dishes.

7 Alla Mascareta
MAP E3 ■ Calle Lunga S Maria
Formosa, Castello 5183 ■ 041 523
07 44 ■ Closed lunch ■ €

An upmarket bar for wine lovers,
Alla Mascareta also serves antipasti
and main dishes.

Alla Mascareta

8 Alle Testiere
MAP E3 ■ Calle del Mondo
Nuovo, Castello 5801 ■ 041 522 72 20
■ Closed Sun & Mon, Aug ■ €€€

There is an unusual selection of
fish, cheese and wines at this tiny,
cosy restaurant.

9 Le Spighe
MAP G4 ■ Via Giuseppe
Garibaldi, Castello 1341
■ 041 523 81 73 ■ Closed Sun ■ €

A great vegan and vegetarian eatery
and food emporium, Le Spighe is a
must for those who don't eat meat.

10 Al Covo
MAP F4 ■ Campiello de la
Pescaria, Castello 3968 ■ 041 522
38 12 ■ Closed Wed & Thu, 1 week
Aug, 4 weeks Dec–Jan ■ €€€

Come here for sophisticated fish
dishes and pair them with choices
from the Italian wine list.

See map on pp108–9 ←

🔟 The Northern Lagoon

The northern lagoon is dotted with mud flats and abandoned islands where rambling monasteries lie crumbling in the sun, backed by sweeping views of snow-capped mountains. Refugees from the mainland, fleeing the Huns, first settled on Torcello, which grew with the additional influx of influential religious orders. Today, however, only a handful of islands are still inhabited – glassmaking Murano is the most important, while

Burano, Mazzorbo and Sant'Erasmo have skeletal populations of fishermen and market gardeners. Salt pans, such as Le Saline, were a source of employment until as late as 1913.

Glass birds on Murano

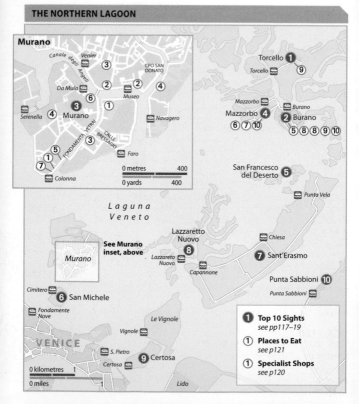

THE NORTHERN LAGOON

Murano

Canale degli Angeli
Venier ③
CPO SAN DONATO
Da Mula ② ② ④
⑥ ① Museo
Serenella ④ ③ ④ Murano
Navagero
CALLE BRESSAGIO
FONDAMENTA VETRAI
③ Faro
① ⑤
⑦
Colonna

0 metres 400
0 yards 400

Torcello ①
Torcello ⑨

Mazzorbo
Mazzorbo ④
Burano
② Burano
⑥⑦⑩ ⑤⑧⑧⑨⑩

San Francesco ⑤
del Deserto

Punta Vela

Laguna Veneto

Lazzaretto Nuovo
⑧
Lazzareto Nuovo
Capannone
Chiesa
Sant'Erasmo ⑦

Punta Sabbioni ⑩
Punta Sabbioni

See Murano inset, above
Murano

Cimitero ⑥ San Michele
Fondamente Nove

Le Vignole
Vignole

VENICE
S. Pietro
Certosa ⑨
Certosa

0 kilometres 1
0 miles

Lido

① **Top 10 Sights**
see pp117–19

① **Places to Eat**
see p121

① **Specialist Shops**
see p120

Previous pages Cappella degli Scrovegni, Padua

1
Torcello
See pp36–7.

2
Burano
MAP H1 ■ Ferry No. 12 from Fondamente Nuove or S Zaccaria
A haven for artists, Burano takes pride in its brightly painted houses, fish and lace-making. The islanders cherish an old legend about a faithful sailor who resisted the Sirens' call and was rewarded with a magnificent veil of magical foam for his bride, later worked into lace, a trade that brought worldwide fame and fortune to the isolated fisherfolk. These days, old women still strain their eyes with patient stitches, but many articles are imported from abroad. The island's dramatically leaning bell tower is visible from afar.

3
Murano
MAP G2 ■ Vaporetto lines 4.1 & 4.2 from Fondamente Nuove & S Zaccaria, 3 from P Roma or seasonal lines
Long synonymous with glassmaking, Murano brought blowing and fusion techniques to extraordinary heights in the 1500s, and so closely guarded were the trade secrets that skilled craftsmen could migrate only under pain of death. Though Venice's glass monopoly lasted only until the 17th century, its fame lives on. A visit to the Glass Museum (Museo del Vetro) with its 4,000 exhibits is a must (see p54). Don't be put off by the reps who invite tourists to see a furnace and showroom; it's a unique opportunity to watch the glassblowers at work and is free. However, if you accept a free boat trip from San Marco to a glass factory, you're expected to make your own way back by *vaporetto* if you don't buy anything. Glassmaking aside, Murano is a lovely place with canals, alleyways and friendly islanders.

4
Mazzorbo
MAP H1 ■ Ferry No. 12 from Fondamente Nuove
This pretty, verdant island exudes a tranquil air as locals tend their vineyards or artichoke fields.

Wicker cages for fattening up *moleche* (soft-shelled crabs) hang over the water and the produce can be sampled in the low-key trattorias. Amid the scattering of houses are bold modern council blocks, which are painted in pastel hues. Mazzorbo has its own boat stop but is also joined to Burano by a long timber footbridge.

Quaint waterfront of Mazzorbo

5
San Francesco del Deserto
MAP H1 ■ Taxi launch from Burano's landing stage ■ Monastery: open 9–11am, 3–5pm Tue–Sun ■ Donation ■ www.sanfrancescodeldeserto.it
A short distance from Burano, this attractive island of cypress trees is home to a Franciscan monastery. According to legend it was founded by St Francis in person, on his way back from preaching missions in Egypt and Palestine in 1220. In May, clad in their brown habits and sandals, the monks attend the Vogalonga regatta (see p76) in their heavy-duty boat, much to the delight of the Venetian crowds.

San Francesco del Deserto

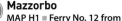

San Michele cemetery

6 San Michele

MAP G2 ■ Ferry Nos. 4.1 &
4.2 from Fondamente Nove &
S Zaccaria ■ Cemetery: open 7:30am–
6pm daily (closes 4pm Oct–Mar)

San Michele became the city
cemetery in 1826, in the wake of a
Napoleonic decree that the dead
should be buried far from city
dwellings to improve hygiene
standards. Entry to the cemetery is
via a lovely Gothic portal surmounted
by St Michael at odds with a dragon,
and through the monk's colonnaded
cloister. But don't neglect to visit the
pretty marble-façaded church next
door, designed by Mauro Coducci
(see p55) in 1469. On All Souls' Day
(2 November), the place is crowded
with relatives paying a visit to their
dear departed. However, unless
you're a famous resident like Ezra
Pound, Igor Stravinsky or Sergei
Diaghilev, your bones are dug up
after 10 years and placed in an urn
to make room for someone else.

7 Sant'Erasmo

MAP H2 ■ Ferry No. 13 from
Fondamente Nuove

Just over 4 km (2.5 miles) long and
1 km (0.5 miles) at the broadest
point, Sant'Erasmo offers tranquil
countryside, praised enthusiastically
by the Romans who built sumptuous
villas here. A couple of rickety old
motorcars occasionally bump along
the lanes, but bicycles and boats
are still the main form of transport.
The main activity here is market
gardening, particularly the
production of delicious asparagus
and artichokes, which prosper on
the sandy soil and are a mainstay of
Rialto Market (see p34). There is also
a small stretch of sandy beach.

Asparagus and artichokes

8 Lazzaretto Nuovo

MAP H2 ■ Ferry No. 13 from
Fondamente Nuove ■ Tours Apr–Oct:
9:45am & 4:30pm Sat & Sun
■ www.lazzarettonuovo.com

Up until the 1700s this island, across
the water from Sant'Erasmo, served
as a quarantine station for merchant
ships entering the lagoon and
suspected of carrying the plague.
Together with Sant'Erasmo it held
up to 10,000 people during the
1576 pestilence, while cargoes
were fumigated with rosemary and
juniper in temporary shelters. Later
converted into a military stronghold,

LAGOON FLORA AND FAUNA

The lagoon abounds in gilt-head
bream, sea bass, clams, cuttlefish and
crabs, all prey for wetland waterfowl
such as swans, egrets (**below**),
cormorants and the rare black-winged
stilts. Sea lavender blooms on land
masses, rock samphire clings to
crumbling masonry, while glasswort
thrives in the salt-ridden marshes.

it now swarms with archaeology enthusiasts, intent on unearthing its secrets, and Italian students attending summer camps.

9 Certosa
MAP H2

Inhabited by religious communities for more than 600 years, the "charterhouse" island went the way of many of its neighbours under occupation by French, Austrian and Italian forces, though currently as the property of the City Council it is slowly being cleaned up as a public park. It can be visited in summer months, though opening times vary; Alilaguna Blu boats (see p139) stop here seasonally. From the Lido–Punta Sabbioni ferry the impressive ramparts of Sanmicheli's 16th-century Forte di Sant'Andrea can be seen, much as they must have appeared in the past to any hostile vessels that dared to enter the lagoon unbidden.

10 Punta Sabbioni
Ferry No. 14 from Lido & S Zaccaria

This locality clings to the promontory extending westward from the mainland – a continuous string of beach resorts equipped with spacious campsites. Alongside sleepy backwaters and canals is Punta Sabbioni ("big sandy point"), a busy bus-ferry terminal that bustles with summer holiday-makers. It came into being as sand accumulated behind the 1,100-m (3,600-ft) breakwater erected to protect the port mouth and littoral. The stretch offers lovely seaside strolls.

Punta Sabbioni

SAILING THE LAGOON

▶ MORNING

To save money, buy a one-day travel card and then take a *vaporetto* to **Murano** (see p117) to watch a glassmaking demonstration at a furnace or one of the workshops. Don't miss Murano's very own **Grand Canal**, before returning via Fondamenta Manin with its medieval porticoes for the turn-off towards the **Faro** (lighthouse) landing stage. Bar al Faro is a perfect place for coffee (Fondamenta Piave 20, Murano; 041 739 724).

Take a ferry to **Burano** (see p117). Either picnic on the famous Burano biscuits or lunch at Da Romano (Piazza Galuppi 221, Burano; 041 730 030; closed Tue & Sun dinner, mid-Dec–early Feb), a popular meeting place for artists.

AFTERNOON

Pop over to **Torcello** (see pp36–7) by ferry for the awe-inspiring Byzantine mosaics in the basilica. Climb the bell tower for views of the lagoon and the Dolomite mountains, if weather conditions and visibility are favourable.

Take the ferry back to Burano and then head east, past low-lying islands and tidal flats towards Treporti. A stretch parallel to the sandy littoral separating the lagoon from the Adriatic Sea takes you to **Punta Sabbioni**, where a stopover is feasible for a drink on the jetty.

End the day sailing across the broad lagoon mouth, via the **Lido** (see p123), back to **Piazza San Marco** (see pp20–23).

See map on p116 ←

Specialist Shops

1 ### Cesare Sent
MAP G2
- Fondamenta
Vetrai 8B, Murano

This talented artist from a long line of glassmakers transforms the ancient art of murrhine glassware into striking modern objects of beauty.

Cesare Sent glasswork

2 ### ArtStudio
MAP G2

- Fondamenta Rivalonga 48, Murano

Watch glass artist Davide Penso at work producing marvellous African-inspired glass beads.

3 ### Manin 56
MAP G2 - Fondamenta Manin 56, Murano

Striking etched bowls and slender wine glasses from Salviati flank international designer items in this wonderful collection.

4 ### Nason & Moretti
MAP G2 - Calle Dietro Gli Orti 12, Murano

This small shop stocks a stunning collection of glassware created by these acclaimed Murano designers in a dazzling array of colours and styles. It is well worth visiting.

5 ### Barovier & Toso
MAP G2 - Fondamenta Vetrai 28, Murano

The oldest family of glassmakers in the world, the Baroviers are able to trace their ancestry back to the 13th century. They still produce stunning contemporary pieces.

6 ### Mazzega
MAP G2 - Fondamenta da Mula 147, Murano

Vast showrooms at Mazzega display traditional and semimodern glass designs, with an emphasis on chandeliers and vases.

7 ### CAM
MAP G2 - Piazzale Colonna 1, Murano

This is the first shop visitors see as they disembark at the Murano Colonna stop. It is an internationally known firm specializing in distinctive high-quality, modern pieces.

8 ### Pastificio e Panificio Giorgio Garbo
MAP H1 - Via S Mauro 336, Burano

Sample some *bussolai*, Burano's trademark vanilla-flavoured shortbread, freshly baked in traditional rounds or "S" shapes.

9 ### Emilia Burano
MAP H1 - Via Galuppi 205, Burano

Superb laceware and exquisite in-house designed linen collections are sold at this family-run boutique.

10 ### Lidia Merletti d'Arte
MAP H1 - Via Galuppi 215, Burano

While the front of this shop is an emporium of lace tablecloths, hand towels and mats, the rear has a gallery with a priceless 18th-century wedding gown, a lace fan owned by Louis XIV and lace altarpieces.

Lidia Merletti d'Arte

Places to Eat

1 Trattoria Busa alla Torre, Da Lele

MAP G2 ▪ Campo S Stefano 3, Murano
▪ 041 739 662 ▪ Open for lunch only
▪ €

Dine inside under timber rafters or
out in the square. Start with ravioli
filled with fish, but leave room for the
nougat pastries.

2 Panificio Giovanni Marcato

MAP G2 ▪ Fondamenta Rivalonga 16,
Murano ▪ 041 739 176 ▪ Closed Sun
▪ €

Pizza with tomato and olives, *zaletti*
biscuits and *pincetto* (sponge cake
with chocolate) feature on the menu.

3 Osteria La Perla Ai Bisatei

MAP G2 ▪ Campo S Bernardo 6,
Murano ▪ 041 739 528 ▪ Open for
lunch only ▪ No credit cards ▪ €

The *fritto misto* seafood is superb at
this restaurant offering home-style
cooking at reasonable prices.

4 Trattoria Valmarana

MAP G2 ▪ Fondamenta
Navagero 31, Murano ▪ 041 739 313
▪ Open for lunch daily & Fri & Sat
dinner ▪ €

Rombo al forno con patate e olive
(flounder with potatoes and olives) is
a speciality at this stylish restaurant
with a waterside terrace.

5 Riva Rosa Ristorante

MAP H1 ▪ Via S Mauro 296,
Burano ▪ 041 730 850 ▪ Open for
lunch Thu–Tue & May–Sep: Sat dinner
(booking essential) ▪ €€€

Try the Rossini *aperitivo* with freshly
juiced strawberries and Prosecco at
this romantic canalside eatery.

6 Trattoria ai Cacciatori

MAP H1 ▪ Fondamenta S
Caterina 24, Mazzorbo ▪ 041 730 848
▪ Open for lunch only ▪ Closed Mon ▪ €

Here you can savour local seafood
such as crab with potato dumplings
and, in autumn, local game.

Antica Trattoria alla Maddalena

7 Antica Trattoria alla Maddalena

MAP H1 ▪ Fondamenta S Caterina 7B,
Mazzorbo ▪ 041 730 151 ▪ Open for
lunch and early dinner (booking
essential); closed Thu, Jan ▪ €

Try the spring artichokes or the roast
duck with a light, local white wine at
this superb restaurant.

8 Al Gatto Nero

MAP H1 ▪ Fondamenta
Giudecca 88, Burano ▪ 041 730 120
▪ Closed Mon, 1st week Jul, 2 weeks
in Nov ▪ €€

This alfresco fish restaurant serves
fresh seafood and homemade pasta.

9 Locanda Cipriani

MAP H1 ▪ Piazza S Fosca 29,
Torcello ▪ 041 730 150 ▪ Closed Nov–
Dec: Mon & Tue; Jan–Feb ▪ €€€

The house speciality here is *filetto di
San Pietro Carlina* (baked John Dory
with tomato and capers).

10 Venissa

MAP H1 ▪ Fondamenta
S Caterina 3, Mazzorbo ▪ 041 527
22 81 ▪ Closed Nov–Feb (restaurant)
▪ €–€€€

Choose between the low-key *osteria*
and the sophisticated restaurant
serving locally grown produce.

See map on pp116

🔟 The Southern Lagoon and Venice Lido

The southern lagoon enjoys protection from the Adriatic Sea with shifting sand spits long transformed into a permanent littoral, the residential Lido, with the help of nature and man. The latter's efforts date back to the 6th century, but the earth and wicker barriers have since been modified into sturdy seawalls and massive parallel breakwaters at the shipping entrances of San Nicolò, Alberoni and Chioggia. On the lagoon's southwestern edge are fish farms and wild shallows where hunters and fishermen still roam, well clear of the Valle Averto reserve run by the World Wildlife Fund for Nature (WWF). Closer to Venice itself is a cluster of sizeable islands such as majestic San Giorgio and populous Giudecca, then diminutive land masses such as Lazzaretto Vecchio, where plague victims were once quarantined but which has now been re-adapted as a home for stray dogs, a sanatorium acquired for private development as an exclusive resort, and countless other evocative abandoned places.

Chiesa del Santissimo Redentore, Giudecca

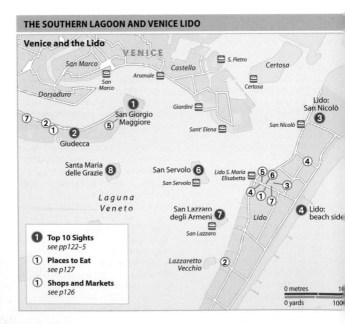

THE SOUTHERN LAGOON AND VENICE LIDO

Interior of San Giorgio Maggiore

1 San Giorgio Maggiore
**Fondazione Giorgio Cini
(vaporetto No. 2)** ■ Open 10am–5pm
(to 4pm Oct–Apr) Sat & Sun for guided
visits (book ahead: 338 683 46 01 or
347 338 64 26) ■ Adm

The island of cypresses is separated
from the main body of Venice by
St Mark's Basin and retains a quiet,
meditative air. An ancient vineyard and
salt pans were replaced by a landmark
church by Andrea Palladio (see p55),
adjoining an elegant Benedictine
monastery. It is now a scientific and
cultural foundation and conference
centre. At the rear is the
open-air Teatro Verde,
which is used for perfor-
mances of contemporary
dance and music.

2 Giudecca
**Vaporetto Nos. 2,
4.1, 4.2**

An S-shaped slice of
land facing the sun-
blessed Zattere, this
residential garden
island was first known as "Spina
longa" for its fishbone form. It was
renamed either after an early Jewish
community or the *giudicati* (radical
aristocrats) exiled here. Italian
Renaissance artist Michelangelo
spent three peaceful years here
in voluntary exile from 1529. Much
later it became an important
industrial zone with shipbuilding
and the immense Molino Stucky
flour mill. Usually quiet and
neighbourly, it comes to life with
a vengeance for the mid-July
Redentore festivities (see p76).

3 Lido: San Nicolò
**Jewish Cemetery: Bus A from
S Maria Elisabetta or car ferry from
Tronchetto** ■ Guided visits to the
cemetery Mar–Oct (book ahead: 041
715 359) ■ www.museoebraico.it

The northern end of the Lido littoral,
a key point in the Republic's defence,
used to be equipped with impressive
naval fortifications, and chains would
be laid across the lagoon mouth as
a deterrent to invaders. The historic
Festa della Sensa celebration (see p77)
is held offshore from the church of
San Nicolò, founded in 1044 and a
former Benedictine monastery, now
a study centre. One visitable
site is the 1386 Jewish
cemetery. Alternatively,
take a 35-minute mini
cruise on the car ferry
between Tronchetto
car park and San
Nicolò. Its high decks
offer great views.

The Southern Lagoon

Fusina
Venice
Lido
Area shown
on map, left

Laguna
Veneto

3

5 Malamocco

Alberoni

Golfo di
Venezia

6 9 San Pietro in Volta

9 Pellestrina

8 9 10
8 9 10
10 Chioggia

0 km   3
0 miles   3

San Nicolò, Lido

dwindled in 1725 it was given over to a sanatorium for psychiatric cases, although exclusively those of "comfortable circumstances". The roomy buildings are now shared by an international university and a trade school for artisans from all over Europe interested in restoration of stone and stucco techniques.

Student painting at San Servolo

4 Lido: Beach Side
Ferry Nos. 1, 5.1, 5.2, 6, 14

Manicured sand, raked daily, and neat rows of multicoloured bathing cabins and beach umbrellas sum up the Lido from June to September, made famous in Thomas Mann's novel *Death in Venice (see p52)*. Venetians spend their summers socializing in style here. Things liven up considerably for the 10-day International Film Festival in September *(see p64)*, when the shady streets are filled with film buffs and critics on bicycles.

5 Lido: Malamocco
Bus No. 11 or line B from S Maria Elisabetta

About midway along the Lido is the pretty, quiet village of Malamocco and it's now hard to imagine that it was the most important lagoon settlement soon after Roman times and the main port for Padua. A storm and giant waves washed away the entire town in 1106, but it was later rebuilt in the vicinity on a smaller scale. It is appreciated for its 15th-century buildings, peaceful nature and rustic trattorias.

6 San Servolo
Ferry No. 20 from San Zaccaria
■ Open 10:45am–2pm Mon–Thu, 3:30–6:30pm Fri, 11:30am–6:30pm Sat & Sun and for guided visits (book ahead: 331 172 87 91) ■ Adm

In 1648, 200 nuns exiled from Candia, Crete, by the Turks were lodged on this island, but after their numbers

7 San Lazzaro degli Armeni
Ferry line No. 20 from San Zaccaria
■ 041 526 01 04 ■ Open 3:20–5pm daily ■ Adm

Venice made a gift of this erstwhile leper colony to the Armenian monk, the Venerable Mechtar, forced out

San Lazzaro degli Armeni

of the Peloponnese during one of his country's diasporas. Intent on fostering the Armenian culture and language, he founded a religious community here and set up a printing press that ran until 1994. Multilingual monks instruct visitors in Armenian history and lead tours through a small museum and a library of more than 100,000 volumes and precious illuminated manuscripts.

8 Santa Maria delle Grazie
Close to San Giorgio, this abandoned island used to be a hospice for pilgrims and was named after a miraculous image of the Virgin brought back from Constantinople and attributed to St Luke. Its colourful history features a series of religious orders and

churches, devastating fires, allotments, luxuriant gardens and the city's infectious diseases hospital. It is now private property with no public access.

⑨ San Pietro in Volta and Pellestrina

Bus-ferry No. 11 from the Lido or from Chioggia

This narrow 11-km (6.5-mile) central strip of land, linked to the Lido and Chioggia by ferry, is dotted with picturesque sleepy fishing communities, once famous for lacemaking and now renowned for champion rowers and a shipyard. The Genoese wiped out the villages during the 14th century, an event almost repeated during the disastrous 1966 floods – powerful waves broke over the seawall, forcing full-scale evacuation. The massive defensive barriers with their 14-m (46-ft) broad base were first erected in the 1700s, but have consequently needed large-scale reinforcement.

⑩ Chioggia

Ferry from Pellestrina or bus from Piazzale Roma

A lively fishing town, Chioggia has elegant bridges over navigable canals. The friendly inhabitants have a reputation for lawlessness and bickering, and speak a distinctive dialect with a singsong inflection. Chioggia's greatest moment came as the arena for the decisive battle in the 1378–9 war, when the Genoese came close to conquering Venice. In flat-bottomed boats the crafty locals lured the enemy into the lagoon, thus gaining the upper hand.

Cleaning fishing nets in Chioggia

A DAY ON THE LAGOON

▶ MORNING

From the Santa Maria Elisabetta ferry stop, either hire a bicycle or take bus B southwest along the lagoon edge for **Malamocco**. Wander through the peaceful village and over its bridge to the sea to take in the Adriatic and the impressive seawall. Then proceed with buses B or 11 through **Alberoni** and past the golf course for the vehicle ferry across the lagoon entrance. Get off at the second stop for **San Pietro in Volta**. Climb the high seawall for panoramic views of the sea, before turning lagoon-wards for the picturesque pastel-painted fishing settlement that spreads along the waterfront.

Have lunch at one of the trattorias (see p127) or a sandwich and glass of wine at one of the modest waterfront bars.

AFTERNOON

Further south the bus terminates at **Pellestrina**, a brightly painted fishing village flanked by an active shipyard. The passenger ferry to **Chioggia** is a beautiful half-hour cruise past mussel grounds punctuated with fisher huts perched on poles, via the Ca' Roman landing stage, which provides access to a beach. Chioggia is a lovely town to explore, with its traffic-free piazza lined with old palazzos and countless fish restaurants.

Indulge in a pre-dinner drink and some *cicchetti* (bar snacks) at one of the laid-back cafés in the elegant Corso del Popolo.

See map on pp122–3

Shops and Markets

Rizzo delicatessen

1 Rizzo
MAP H2 ■ Gran Viale Santa
Maria Elisabetta 16/20, Lido

This stocks unbeatable gourmet
food from all over Italy – buffalo
mozzarella, creamy Asiago cheese,
cured Parma ham and gleaming
olives. Pizza and focaccia can be
found at the bread counter.

2 General Market
MAP H2 ■ Via Falier, Lido
■ Tue am

Open-sided vans sell fresh produce,
alongside designer-quality clothes,
shoes and bags at reasonable prices.
Even if you don't buy anything, the
lagoon setting looking over to the
Venice skyline makes a trip to this
market worthwhile.

3 Erbalido
MAP H2 ■ Via Negroponte
4/C, Lido

Here you will find a traditional
herbalist who can advise on natural
remedies for minor ailments.

4 Arbor
MAP H2 ■ Gran Viale Santa
Maria Elisabetta 10, Lido

The upmarket range of menswear
and womenswear at this clothes
shop attracts both foreign and
Italian customers.

5 Lido on Bike
MAP H2 ■ Gran Viale Santa
Maria Elisabetta 21/B, Lido

This well-stocked bike shop rents
out all normal steeds as well as
4-wheeler family models.

6 OVS Conad
MAP H2 ■ Gran Viale Santa
Maria Elisabetta 21/B, Lido

A store with fashionable, moderately
priced clothing for all ages is
combined with a supermarket with
a great selection of fresh produce.

7 Benetton
MAP H2 ■ Gran Viale Santa
Maria Elisabetta 47/A, Lido

Despite being small, this shop
is well-stocked with underwear,
nightwear and swimwear.

8 El Penelo
MAP F2 ■ 577 Borgo San
Giovanni, Chioggia

Giorgio Boscolo is an expert in
crafting traditional fishermen's clay
pipes – and he is the only craftsman
who still makes them in terracotta
and coloured glazes.

9 Venturini Souvenirs
MAP F1 ■ Corso del Popolo
1349, Chioggia

Ignore the trinkets here and instead
focus on the intricately hand-crafted
models of *bragozzo* boats (see p26).

Venturini Souvenirs

10 Panificio Sergio
MAP F1 ■ Stradale Ponte
Caneva 626, Chioggia

The dry biscuits sold here were
traditionally made for seafarers.
Pevarini are spicy rings with
molasses and aniseed, while
Dolce del Doge is spread with a
chocolate-hazelnut mixture.

Places to Eat

PRICE CATEGORIES
For a three-course meal for one with half a bottle of wine (or equivalent meal), taxes and extra charges.

€ under €40   €€ €40–60   €€€ over €60

1 Altanella

MAP E6 ▪ Calle delle Erbe, Giudecca 268 ▪ 041 522 77 80 ▪ Closed Mon & Tue, Dec & Jan, 10–20 Aug ▪ €€€

Treat yourself to a candlelit dinner on the terrace. Fish dishes such as *frittura mista* (assorted fried seafood) are the speciality.

2 Ai Cacciatori
MAP D6 ▪ Fondamenta Ponte Piccolo Giudecca 320 ▪ 041 528 58 49 ▪ Closed Mon, 15 Dec–15 Jan ▪ €€€

Enjoy hearty Venetian fare such as *gnocchi con nero di seppia* (potato dumplings with cuttlefish ink) in canal-side seating with lovely views.

3 Trattoria Scarso
MAP H2 ▪ Piazzale Malamocco 5, Malamocco ▪ 041 770 834 ▪ Closed Mon dinner, Tue, Jan, Nov ▪ €

The good-value family-run Trattoria Scarso has a lovely garden hung with fishing nets where you can linger over grilled fish or a fresh salad.

4 Trattoria La Favorita
MAP H2 ▪ Via Francesco Duodo 33, Lido ▪ 041 526 16 26 ▪ Closed Mon ▪ €€

Run by the same family for many years, this exemplary traditional fish restaurant is a firm favourite with both locals and discerning visitors.

5 Hotel Cipriani
MAP E6 ▪ Giudecca 10 ▪ 041 240 801 ▪ Closed Nov–Mar ▪ €€€

Savour an artistic tasting menu at Michelin-starred Oro Restaurant, sip a mocktail at Cip's Club, or have a rustic dinner at Giudecca 10, Hotel Cipriani *(see p68)* is the perfect venue for every mood.

6 Ristorante da Memo
Via Portosecco 157, S Pietro in Volta ▪ 041 527 91 25 ▪ Closed Tue, Nov–Mar ▪ €€

Try the fresh shrimps, eel or sole at this modest seafood restaurant with outdoor tables.

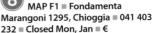
Excellent view from Harry's Dolci

7 Harry's Dolci
MAP C6 ▪ Fondamenta S. Biagio, Giudecca 773 ▪ 041 522 48 44 ▪ Closed Nov–Easter ▪ €€€

With views across the Giudecca Canal, this is the "sweet" branch of Harry's Bar *(see p25)*, for sorbets and pastries.

8 Ristorante La Sgura
MAP F1 ▪ Fondamenta Marangoni 1295, Chioggia ▪ 041 403 232 ▪ Closed Mon, Jan ▪ €

Situated on a quiet canal, this place also has a great selection of meat. Try the *zuppa di pesce* (fish soup).

9 Ristorante El Gato
MAP F1 ▪ Corso del Popolo 653, Chioggia ▪ 041 400 265 ▪ Closed Mon, 15–28 Feb ▪ €€

With a long-standing reputation for excellence, this restaurant serves superb *frittura* (fried fish), fish risotto and sautéed mussels and clams.

10 Ristorante al Buon Pesce
MAP F1 ▪ Stradale Ponte Caneva 625, Chioggia ▪ 041 400 861 ▪ Closed Wed ▪ €

A range of delicious fresh grilled fish and fried seafood is available at this spacious, friendly fish restaurant.

See map on pp122–3

TOP10 Padua, Vicenza and Verona

A wealth of art cities punctuates the fertile Veneto plain that stretches in a broad wedge north from the Po River to the foothills of the Dolomites. There is evidence of the presence of Romans and Venetians alike in the shape of fascinating amphitheatres and elegant palaces in cities such as Verona and Vicenza, both of which have been declared World Heritage Sites by UNESCO. Moreover, amid vineyards of grapes, pressed for light sparkling Prosecco and aromatic Bardolino, are charming, little-visited villas with ornamental gardens. Each town has its distinctive character: Padua, a business hub but with a richly artistic and religious heart; Vicenza, famous for its goldsmiths and Andrea Palladio's architecture; and romantic Verona, lazing on the banks of the mighty Adige River as it flows south swollen with snow-melt from the Alps. The highlights in each city can easily be visited as day-trips from Venice by train.

Piazza dei Signori

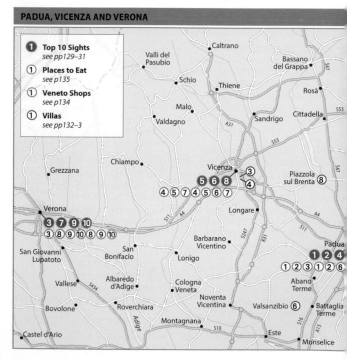

PADUA, VICENZA AND VERONA

- **1** Top 10 Sights
  see pp129–31
- **1** Places to Eat
  see p135
- **1** Veneto Shops
  see p134
- **1** Villas
  see pp132–3

Fresco in the Cappella degli Scrovegni

① Cappella degli Scrovegni
Piazza Eremitani, Padua
■ Bus Nos. 3, 10, 12 ■ 049 201 00 20
■ Open 9am–7pm daily (booking essential) ■ Adm ■ www.cappella degliscrovegni.it

The sky-blue vault studded with gold stars in this glorious Paduan chapel seems to hover over Giotto's vibrant frescoes, which narrate the lives of Mary and Jesus. The Florentine artist (1266–1337) was summoned by Enrico Scrovegni to work on the chapel in 1305–6, to atone for the sins of his late father, a moneylender. Especially noteworthy among the 38 distinct scenes is the *Last Judgment* on the entrance wall, with its ranks of helmeted, haloed and shield-bearing angels. Book well in advance in summer. Visits last 30–35 minutes, including a 15-minute wait in the "decontamination" chamber.

② Palazzo Bo
Via VIII Febbraio 2, Padua
■ Bus Nos. 3, 12 ■ 049 827 39 39
■ Guided tours: Mon–Fri & Sat am
■ Adm ■ www.unipd.it

The original lectern where Galileo Galilei held his lessons between 1592 and 1610 can be seen on the guided tour of Padua's historic university, founded in 1222 and second only to Bologna as Italy's and the world's oldest. The institution boasts the world's first anatomy theatre (1594) where dissections had to be carried out in great secrecy as the church forbade such practices. Other illustrious scholars of the university have included astronomer Copernicus (1473–1543), Gabriel Falloplus (1523–62), who discovered the function of the Fallopian tubes, and Elena Lucrezia Corner Piscopia *(see p50)*, the world's first woman graduate.

The 16th-century anatomy theatre in Padua's University

ROMEO AND JULIET

There is no doubt that the Capulet and Montague families existed, though they were probably more friendly than William Shakespeare made out in his 1594–5 tragedy. However, the world's most famous star-crossed lovers may have come from Vicenza, the home town of Luigi Da Porto, author of the original 1530 account.

3 Casa di Giulietta
Via Cappello 23, Verona ■ Open 8:30am–7:30pm Tue–Sun, 1:30–7:30pm Mon ■ Adm

Tourists flock to "Juliet's House", the 13th-century presumed abode of the Shakespearean heroine, complete with a pretty balcony (added in 1928) from which you may imagine her uttering that immortal cry: "Romeo, Romeo, wherefore art thou Romeo?" The courtyard walls are filled with multilingual graffiti left by lovers from all over the world.

4 Basilica del Santo
Piazza del Santo, Padua ■ Bus Nos. 3, 18 ■ Open 6:20am–7:45pm daily ■ www.basilicadelsanto.org

Popularly referred to as "il Santo", Padua's revered site of pilgrimage was built in the 13th century to safeguard the mortal remains of St Anthony, a Franciscan monk and miracle worker from Portugal. Devotees visit his gleaming tomb, encircled by burning candles, but his tongue is guarded in an intricate reliquary in the Treasury, recovered after being stolen. Inside you will find artworks by Sansovino, Tiepolo and Titian (see pp54–5).

5 Piazza dei Signori
Basilica Palladiana: Piazza dei Signori, Vicenza ■ Open during exhibitions ■ Adm

In addition to the cafés in Vicenza's main square, visitors can admire the buildings by Palladio, whose 16th-century designs went on to influence both his home town and architecture worldwide (see p55). The basilica has twin levels of colonnaded arches, opposite Palladio's Loggia del Capitaniato. A statue of the architect can be found in the piazzetta at the western end.

6 Palazzo Leoni Montanari
Contra' Santa Corona 25, Vicenza ■ Open 10am–6pm Tue–Sun ■ Adm

On the entrance portal of this lavishly decorated Baroque palace are carvings of writhing serpents, and Hercules is shown in the act of slaying the Hydra on the loggia. The gallery's masterpieces include 120 awe-inspiring Russian icons and 14 fascinating paintings by Pietro Longhi depicting scenes from 18th-century Venetian life.

Juliet statue

7 Verona Arena
Piazza Brà, Verona ■ 045 800 51 51 ■ Open 8:30am–7:30pm daily (times may vary) ■ Adm ■ www.arena.it

This massive Roman amphitheatre dating from the 1st century AD measures almost 140 m (460 ft) in length. The impressive arcades and 44-level tiered seating for 22,000 people, that once rang with the cries of gladiator fights, now echo with arias from operas during the popular summer festival. Verdi's *Aïda* has opened the festival every year since 1913. Visitors should note that the opening hours are shorter during the opera festival in the summer.

Verona Arena

8 Teatro Olimpico
Piazza Matteotti 11, Vicenza
■ Open 9am–5pm Tue–Sun (Jul–Aug: 10am–6pm) ■ Adm

A castle courtyard draped with creepers was chosen for this Vicenza theatre, designed by Palladio and completed by his disciple Vincenzo Scamozzi. The performing area is based on a Roman model, while the stage scenery represents the city of Thebes, built for 1585's inaugural play, Sophocles' *Oedipus Rex*. Scaled statues and varying stage levels create clever tricks of perspective.

Piazza delle Erbe in Verona

9 Piazza delle Erbe
Torre dei Lamberti, Cortile Mercato Vecchio, Verona
■ Open 10am–6pm Mon–Fri, 11am–7pm Sat & Sun ■ Adm

Originally Verona's Roman forum, this square is still a great spot for discussing business over a coffee. Parasols shade souvenirs at the market, watched over by a winged lion atop a column, a vestige of Venetian domination. The 84-m (275-ft) Torre dei Lamberti offers great city views.

10 Museo di Storia Naturale
Lungadige Porta Vittoria 9, Verona
■ Open 9am–5pm Mon–Thu, 2–6pm Sat & Sun ■ Adm

Gigantic ferns, weird fish and an ancestor of the crocodile, all in fossilized form from the Eocene era 50 million years ago, are treasures hailing from Bolca in the Lessini foothills on display here. They testify to the tropical shallows that spread across the area prior to the formation of the Alps.

A DAY OUT IN VERONA

▶ MORNING

Where better to begin than the inspiring **Verona Arena**, where, as entertainment, wild animals once made a meal of gladiators? Afterwards, relax in the sun with a creamy coffee at **Liston 12 Caffè** and dig into a freshly baked jam-filled croissant *(Piazza Brà 12, Verona; 045 803 11 68)*.

A short stroll leads past the boutiques in the traffic-free **Via Mazzini**, paved with pink-tinged local limestone embedded with ammonite fossils, to **Casa di Giulietta** to the right, or **Piazza delle Erbe** and its elegant palaces to the left.

Backtrack to Via Mazzini for lunch at **Ristorante Greppia** *(Vicolo Samaritana 3, Verona; 045 800 45 77; closed Mon)* for *bollito misto* (mixed boiled meat) served with a traditional peppery sauce.

AFTERNOON

To digest lunch, head over the Adige River via the ancient **Ponte di Pietra** to the Roman theatre on Via Rigaste Redentore – well worth a visit even if you're not in town for a summer evening performance. Then follow the river or walk back through town and west towards the medieval **Ponte Scaligero**, part of the adjoining castle. The triple-arched construction was blown up by the German army in World War II, then rebuilt brick by brick by town members.

The bridge leads to **Castelvecchio** for a timely *aperitivo* with a glass of white Soave wine at any of the welcoming bars.

See map on pp128–9 ←

TOP 10 Veneto Villas

1 Villa Barbaro

Via Cornuda 7, Maser, bus from Treviso railway station ■ Open Apr–Oct: 10am–6pm Tue–Sat, 11am–6pm Sun; Nov–Mar: 11am–5pm Sat & Sun ■ Adm ■ www.villadimaser.it

The best preserved villa (1560) by Palladio (see p55) lies close to the pretty hill town of Asolo. This charming country house features all manner of Roman-inspired elements, from the nymphaeum and grotto to the circular temple akin to the Pantheon. Playful trompe l'oeil frescoes by Veronese (see p54) adorn the six main rooms, counting amongst the most important works of art of the Venetian Renaissance, while the garden is punctuated with Classical statuary. Drop in to the estate's wine cellar in a farm house next door for wine tastings.

Villa Barbaro

rooms and a ballroom decorated by Tiepolo (see p54). Above the huge façade columns, scores of statues line the roof overlooking inner court-yards and a spacious park where the Venetian nobility would promenade on sum-mer evenings. Be sure to explore the wonderful 1721 circular maze. The guest list has included one-time proprietor Napoleon, Russian and Austrian royalty, Mussolini and Hitler among others.

3 Villa Valmarana "Ai Nani"

Via dei Nani 8, Vicenza ■ Open Mar–Oct: 10am–6pm daily; Nov–Feb: 10am–4pm daily ■ Adm ■ www.villavalmarana.com

Known for the jaunty statues of dwarfs on the garden wall, these cosy twin buildings, built by the Valmarana family, stand on a pretty ridge looking up to Monte Berico and its sanctuary. The Tiepolo father and son fresco team were invited here by Count Valmarana in 1757 to decorate the main part and the guest quarters.

4 Villa Valmarana "La Rotonda"

Via Rotonda 45, Vicenza (bus No. 8) ■ Villa: open 10am–noon, 3–6pm Wed & Sat (Dec–mid-Mar: 10am–noon, 2:30–5pm); garden: open Tue, Thu, Fri & Sun same hours as villa (times may vary, so check website) ■ Adm ■ www.villalarotonda.it

The perfectly proportioned imposing Villa Valmarana with four temple façades sits on a hill overlooking the architect Palladio's adoptive town of Vicenza. The house has been imitated throughout the world. If you want to visit the villa itself as opposed to the rather limited grounds, beware it's only open two days a week.

Villa Pisani – La Nazionale

2 Villa Pisani – La Nazionale

Via Doge Pisani 7, Strà ■ Villa & park: open 9am–7pm Tue–Sun (Oct–Mar: 9am–4pm); maze: open Apr–Oct ■ Adm ■ www.villapisani.beni culturali.it

This splendid two-floor 18th-century villa designed for Doge Alvise Pisani has 114 sumptuously furnished

⑤ Villa Foscari "La Malcontenta"

Via dei Turisti 9, Malcontenta ▪ Open Apr–Oct: 9am–noon Tue, Wed, Fri & Sat ▪ Adm ▪ www.lamalcontenta.com

Located on the bend of the Brenta Canal, but now rather too close to the Marghera industrial area, this wonderful residence designed by Andrea Palladio in 1571 is one of his best-known creations. It has a Greek temple façade, while the interior is decorated with frescoes. The name is said to refer to the "discontent" of a female member of the Foscari family, exiled here for adultery.

⑥ Villa Barbarigo

Galzignano, Valsanzibio ▪ Open Mar–Nov: 10am–1pm, 2pm–sunset daily ▪ Adm ▪ www.valsanzibiogiardino.it

The Euganean Hills are the setting for this Baroque garden, designed for the Venetian Barbarigo family by Luigi Bernini, architect of the Vatican fountains in Rome. The villa, dating from 1669, is a private dwelling, but the 15-ha (37-acre) garden provides a boxwood maze, fountains, fish ponds, statues and hundreds of trees.

⑦ Villa Emo

Via Stazione 5, Fanzolo di Vedelago ▪ Open Apr–Sep: 10am–6pm daily; Oct–Mar: 10am–5:30pm daily ▪ Adm ▪ www.villaemo.org

Another of Palladio's light-flooded country residences, this villa was built for the Emo family in around 1560. A harmonious central block is flanked by graceful arched

barchesse (wings), designed for storing hay and farm tools. The interior has lively frescoes by Renaissance artist Zelotti, also responsible for the Malcontenta villa decorations.

⑧ Villa Contarini

Piazzola sul Brenta ▪ Open Mar–Oct: 9am–7pm Thu–Tue; Nov–Feb: 10am–4pm Thu–Tue ▪ Adm ▪ www.villacontarini.eu

A horseshoe plaza lined with terraced houses faces the façade of this 17th-century country villa, which was once the focus for a thriving farming community. A remarkable system of acoustics was invented so that musicians performing in the Sala della Musica on the first floor could be clearly heard and appreciated downstairs. An antiques market is held in the grounds on the last Sunday of each month.

⑨ Villa Cornaro

Via Roma 35, Piombino Dese ▪ Open May–Sep: 3:30–6pm Sat ▪ Adm

This unusual, double-tiered creation by Palladio dates to between 1560 and 1570. The façade columns are both Doric and Corinthian in style, with acanthus leaves or scrolls around the capitals. The interior has frescoes by Mattio Borotoloni.

⑩ Barchessa Valmarana

Via Valmarana 11, Mira ▪ Open Mar–Oct: 10am–6pm Tue–Sun; Nov–Feb: 10am–4:30pm Sat & Sun ▪ Adm ▪ www.villaval marana.net

Formerly guest quarters, these are extant "wings" of a 17th-century villa, whose main body was demolished in 1908. Close by are locks on the Brenta waterway, which have been excavated over centuries to divert the river away from the lagoon and eliminate the problem of silting.

Beautiful interior of Villa Emo

See map on pp128–9 ←

Veneto Shops

1 Pasticceria Gelateria Al Duomo
Via Vandelli 2, Padua ■ Closed Tue

This pastry shop has been serving the finest *fritelle* (apple fritters) in town for many decades. It is located on the southern corner of the square by the Duomo.

2 Drogheria ai Due Catini d'Oro Dal Zio
Piazza dei Frutti 46, Padua

Strong mints, peppery Veneto *mostarda* chutney and even feather dusters, among many other things, are sold at this old-fashioned shop.

3 Novella
Via C Cattaneo 18, Verona

Here you will find everything for the female fashionista, created by top Italian designers.

4 Antica Pasticceria di Sorarù
Piazzetta Palladio 17, Vicenza

This inviting pastry shop is lined with tantalizing almond and chocolate delicacies, as well as special goodies such as the dove-shaped *colomba* cake at Easter.

5 Cappelleria Palladio
Piazzetta Palladio 13, Vicenza

Run by a charming couple with a 40-year passion for millinery, this charming old-fashioned shop is a hat-lover's heaven. It is in great demand for stylish weddings in the country villas (see pp132–3).

6 LaFeltrinelli
Via S Francesco 7, Padua

You could occupy yourself for hours by browsing the well-stocked shelves of English- and other European-language crime and mystery novels, fiction, travel, classics, children's literature and reference books in this chain bookshop.

7 Il Ceppo
Corso Palladio 196, Vicenza

A gourmet's paradise, Il Ceppo has mouthwatering takeaway dishes, pickles and preserves. Buy a catered picnic with wine or simply a crusty roll filled with Asiago cheese or *sopressa* sausage.

8 De Rossi "Il Fornaio"
Corso Porta Borsari 3, Verona

A range of pastries and wholemeal breads is available here. Try the *zaletto*, a biscuit baked with pine nuts and sultanas, and of course *Baci di Giulietta* (Juliet's Kisses) – almond paste shaped into pursed lips.

9 Mercante d'Oriente
Corso Sant'Anastasia 34, Verona

Akin to an exotic museum, this antiques dealer dazzles with Chinese and Japanese marvels, Pre-Columbian pieces and traditional and contemporary carpets.

10 Coin
Via Cappello 30, Verona

This wonderful department store with a good range of casual clothes, cosmetics and home furnishings is right in the centre of town.

Antica Pasticceria di Sorarù

Places to Eat

PRICE CATEGORIES
For a three-course meal for one with half a bottle of wine (or equivalent meal), taxes and extra charges.

€ under €40   €€ €40–60   €€€ over €60

Graziati
Piazza della Frutta 40, Padua ▪ €

Light and buttery *millefoglie* pastries perfectly accompany the strong, sweet coffee as you sit outside on the lively market square. Light lunches are served downstairs.

2 Caffè Pedrocchi
Via VIII Febbraio 15, Padua ▪ €

This 1831 Neo-Classical coffee house was long known as the "café without doors" because it never closed. Liberals of the 19th century would meet and argue here, though today it's rather quiet.

Caffè Pedrocchi

3 Osteria dei Fabbri
Via dei Fabbri 13, Padua ▪ 049 650 336 ▪ Closed Sun ▪ €

The appetizing menu at this rustic *osteria* changes daily. Typical dishes include grilled Piedmont cheese with polenta or spare ribs with chicory.

4 Antico Guelfo
Contrà Pedemuro San Biagio 90, Vicenza ▪ 044 454 78 97 ▪ Closed Tue ▪ €€

This central, upmarket restaurant offers more than the usual fare, including superb gluten-free cuisine. It also has an excellent selection of wines. Great value.

Antica Casa della Malvasia
Contrà delle Morette 5, Vicenza ▪ 044 454 37 04 ▪ Closed Sun dinner, Mon, 2 weeks in Jul ▪ €

There is an imaginative menu and vast wine list here. Try the *bigoli all'arna* (spaghetti with duck sauce).

6 Bar Borsa
Piazza dei Signori 26, Vicenza ▪ 044 454 45 83 ▪ Closed Mon lunch

With live music and DJs, hip Borsa attracts a lively crowd. Outdoor seating is on Piazza dei Signori as well as Piazza delle Erbe. It has an all-day menu and offers brunch at weekends.

7 Angolo Palladio
Piazzetta Palladio 12, Vicenza ▪ 044 432 77 90 ▪ Closed Thu lunch ▪ €€

This warm and friendly pizzeria-cum-restaurant serves excellent *baccalà* (salt cod) and boasts an extensive wine list.

8 Ristorante Greppia
Vicolo Samaritana 3, Verona ▪ 045 800 45 77 ▪ Closed Mon, 1–15 Jun ▪ €

The unforgettable Greppia specializes in *bollito misto*, a selection of nine melt-in-the-mouth meats served with peppery *Pearà* sauce.

9 Arche
Via Arche Scaligere 6, Verona ▪ 045 800 74 15 ▪ Closed Mon, Sun dinner, 2 weeks in Jan ▪ €–€€€

Established in 1879, this is one of the best restaurants in Verona. Fish dishes feature strongly on the menu.

10 Bottega del Vino
Vicolo Scudo di Francia 3, Verona ▪ 045 800 45 35 ▪ €€

Dating to 1890, this renowned restaurant holds 2,500 wines in its cellar. The favourite dish among aficionados is *pastissada de caval*, a dark, spicy horse-meat stew.

See map on pp128–9

Streetsmart

Colourful canal houses on Burano

Getting To and Around Venice

Arriving by Air

Marco Polo, Venice's main airport, is 10 km (6.5 miles) north of the city. It is served by many European airlines, including **British Airways** and low-cost carriers **easyJet** and **Jet2**, as well as the national carrier **Alitalia**. London, Frankfurt, Amsterdam and Paris are also transport hubs for Venice. From the US, **Delta Airlines** flies direct from New York, and **American Airlines** flies direct from Philadelphia.

The most exciting way to reach Venice from the airport is by water. The public **Alilaguna** water bus (*vaporetto*) leaves every 15 minutes and takes about an hour. Tickets (€15) are available at the nearby quayside. A water taxi (*motoscafo*) takes about half the time but will cost around €110. The cheaper option is to take a bus to Piazzale Roma. The direct **ATVO Airport bus** (€8) and the **ACTV public bus** No. 5 (€8) leave every 30 minutes. There is a ticket office in the arrivals hall.

Charter flights and low-cost airline **Ryanair** fly into **Antonio Canova Airport** at Treviso, which is 40 km (29 miles) north-west of Venice. To reach Venice from here, take an ATVO Airport Bus to Piazzale Roma (€10), which takes around 50 minutes, or the public bus No. 6 (€1.30) to Treviso station and then continue by train.

Arriving by Sea

Ferries and cruise ships from Greece and Croatia dock at the **Venezia Terminal Passeggeri** near Tronchetto or the San Basilio terminal in western Dorsoduro.

Arriving by Train

The main train operators in Italy are state-owned Alitalia and private **Italo**. Stazione Venezia Santa Lucia is the terminus for trains from the major European cities. Passengers from London need to change in Paris or Ostend. *Vaporetti* connect with all parts of the city from here. Be careful not to get out at Venezia Mestre, the stop before Venice itself. The **Venice Simplon-Orient-Express** from London is a romantic, albeit very costly, way to arrive.

Arriving by Coach

Long-distance and international coaches such as **Eurolines** arrive at Tronchetto, which is four minutes from Piazzale Roma on the People Mover railway shuttle (€1.50).

Arriving by Road

Visitors from EEA/EU countries will need a valid driving licence and credit card to hire a car. Otherwise an International Driving Licence is necessary. Those driving their own car should bring vehicle registration papers and full insurance cover. Italians drive on the right. Since no cars are allowed in Venice, they must be left in one of the large car parks on the outskirts or at the airport. Car parks nearest the city, on Tronchetto or at Piazzale Roma, are more expensive than those at Fusina and San Giuliano near Mestre. Car hire firms such as **Europcar** and **Maggiore** are available at Piazzale Roma and the airport However, it is easy to travel around the Veneto by public transport, except for Venetian Villas. Padua, Vicenza and Verona are all easily accessible on a daytrip by train or bus.

Getting Around by Water

Vaporetti cross and travel the length of the Grand Canal, and are the equivalent of buses in Venice. The most useful route, Line No. 1, makes a leisurely journey (45 minutes) down the Grand Canal from Piazzale Roma to San Marco. Line No. 2 is the Canal's faster route; and Line 12, from Fondamente Nuove, serves the islands of Murano, Burano and Torcello. The service is run by ACTV, and tickets are available at boarding points, bars and tobacconists. There is a flat oneway fare (€7.50), no matter how far you travel. Validate your ticket on the electronic reader before boarding to avoid a hefty fine; you must then start your journey within one hour. Be aware that the stops serve both directions. Most lines run from 5am until midnight, and there is a limited night service. You can buy an ACTV travel card for 1, 2, 3 or 7 days, which you can also load on to the **Venezia Unica** City Pass. The pass can be bought online on the Venezia Unica website.

There are 16 water-taxi ranks from where sleek motor boats (motoscafi), operated by **Consorzio Venezia Taxi, Consorzio Motoscafi** and **Cooperativa Taxi Serenissima**, provide the fastest (but not cheapest) way of getting around. Luggage and waiting cost extra.

Easily recognizable gondoliers await business at the numerous **gondola** ranks. Official rates are €80 for 40 minutes by day, and €100 by night, but establish a price before setting out. Gondolas can take up to six passengers. *Traghetti*, gondola ferries

with an oarsman at each end, cross the Grand Canal (€2) at eight points in daylight. Most residents travel standing up.

Getting Around by Bicycle

Bicycles are banned from the centre, but you can hire a bike for trips on the Lido and Pellestrina, and for excursions out of Venice. **Veloce** arrange customized excursions.

Getting Around on Foot

Venice is a compact city – crossing from north to south only takes around 45 minutes – and, aided by the excellent network of *vaporetti*, which also

travel to the outlying islands, it's easy to see the main sights on foot.

It is also a city where getting lost in the tangle of alleyways (calli) is part of the attraction. Arming yourself with a detailed street map will help you get around, as will the frequent yellow signs on the walls indicating the direction of the main sights. The etiquette of walking is to keep to the right and to keep moving on bridges or in the narrowest alleyways. Once you are out of the San Marco and Rialto districts, however, the flow of tourists becomes much less. The alleyways open out into numerous squares (campi) with benches and cafés.

DIRECTORY

ARRIVING BY AIR

ACTV
☎ 041 24 24
🌐 actv.it

Alilaguna
☎ 041 240 17 01
🌐 alilaguna.it

Alitalia
🌐 alitalia.com

American Airlines
🌐 americanairlines.com

ATVO
☎ 0421 59 44
🌐 atvo.it

British Airways
🌐 britishairways.com

Delta Airlines
🌐 delta.com

easyJet
🌐 easyjet.com

Jet2
🌐 jet2.com

Ryanair
🌐 ryanair.com

Treviso, Antonio Canova
☎ 042 231 51 11
🌐 trevisoairport.it

Venice, Marco Polo
☎ 041 260 92 60
🌐 veniceairport.it

ARRIVING BY SEA

Venezia Terminal Passeggeri
🌐 vtp.it

ARRIVING BY TRAIN

Italo
☎ 06 0708 or +39 06 89371892 from abroad
🌐 italotreno.it

Trenitalia
☎ 89 20 21 or +39 06 684 754 75 from abroad
🌐 trenitalia.com

Venice Simplon-Orient-Express
🌐 belmond.com/ luxury-trains

ARRIVING BY COACH

Eurolines
🌐 eurolines.com

ARRIVING BY ROAD

Europcar
🌐 europcar.it

Maggiore
🌐 maggiore.it

GETTING AROUND BY WATER

Consorzio Motoscafi
☎ 041 522 23 03
🌐 motoscafivenezia.it

Consorzio Venezia Taxi
☎ 328 238 96 61
🌐 veneziataxi.it

Cooperitiva Taxi Serenissima
☎ 800 432 291
🌐 serenissimataxi.it

Gondolas
☎ 041 528 50 75
🌐 gondolavenezia.it

***Vaporetti* (Water Buses)**
☎ 041 2424

Venezia Unica
☎ 041 24 24
🌐 veneziaunica.it

GETTING AROUND BY BICYCLE

Veloce
🌐 rentalbikeitaly.com

Practical Information

Passports and Visas

All visitors to Italy need a valid passport. For residents of the European Union (EU), European Economic Area (EEA), Switzerland, United States, Canada, Australia, New Zealand and Israel visas are required only for stays in excess of 90 days or for those intending to work, but check with your embassy before travelling. The **Italian Foreign Office** also has up-to-date details. Contact your consulate if you lose your passport, need a visa or wish to stay longer than 90 days.

Most countries have consular representation in Italy including **Australia**, **Canada**, **New Zealand**, **UK** and the **US**.

Customs and Immigration

Allowances for visitors for personal use, from the EU are almost unlimited. If you need medication, bring enough and keep a copy of your prescription. Check **Customs Information** website for allowances outside and within the EU.

Travel Safety Advice

Visitors can get up-to-date travel safety information from the **UK Foreign and Commonwealth Office**, the **US Department of State** and the **Australian Department of Foreign Affairs and Trade**.

Travel Insurance

It's advisable to take out an insurance policy to cover cancellation or curtailment of your trip, theft, loss of money and baggage, and healthcare, including repatriation. Visitors from EU/EEA countries should bring a European Health Insurance Card (EHIC) which will give free or reduced healthcare including pre-existing medical conditions and routine maternity care, but will not cover repatriation.

Health

For urgent medical aid, go to the emergency (*pronto soccorso*) department of the **Ospedale SS Giovanni e Paolo** in Castello. For ambulance (*ambulanza*), dial 118. There are First Aid Points for tourists, open 8am to 8pm daily, in Piazza San Marco and Piazzale Roma. The **Health Venice** website lists doctors and pharmacies, and your hotel or a tourist office can give contact numbers for night doctors and dentists.

Pharmacies (*farmacie*) tend to open 9am–12.30pm and 4–7.30pm Monday to Friday, and 9am–noon on Saturdays. A rota (*farmacie di turno*) of night-time and Sunday opening is posted online and on pharmacy doors. The *Un Ospite di Venezia* booklet (see p143) also has this information. Italian pharmacists are trained to deal with minor ailments.

No inoculations are needed. Take a high-factor sunscreen in summer. An insect repellent and an electric plug-in insect killer will help guard against mosquitoes. It is safe to drink tap water and water from fountains unless you see the sign *non potabile* (not drinkable).

Personal Security

Venice is a safe city, but still has its share of pickpockets. Leave important documents and valuables in a hotel safe and only carry the money you need. Be extra vigilant at train stations, markets, on public transport, at the landing stages of the *vaporetti* – especially while boarding. Venice is safe at night, and women alone should encounter no trouble. Make sure you only use official taxis, or you may be overcharged.

In the event of a theft, report it at the nearest **Questura** (police station) and take your passport. But if you have lost your passport, consult your consulate immediately. In any emergency, call 118 for assistance (*pronto soccorso*); or call 113 for the police (*Polizia di Stato*) or 115 for the fire brigade (*Vigili del Fuoco*). If you leave anything on a train, contact the **City Lost Property**. Items left on *vaporetti* are kept at the **ACTV Lost Property** (*Oggetti Smarriti*) offices (7:30am–7:30pm daily) in Piazzale Roma for a week.

Travellers with Specific Needs

For travellers with specific needs, the Venezia Accessibile information pack, available on the **Sanitrans** website or at tourist offices, details the best way of getting around the 70 per cent of Venice. It lists barrier-free itineraries, arrangements for arriving by train, air and bus, public toilets, car parks, manageable bridges and travelling by *vaporetto* or *motoscafo*. It also lists shops where you can hire lightweight wheelchairs. Travellers can buy discounted single-fare tickets for the *vaporetti*, which last 75 minutes and allow a companion to travel free.

Museums and churches are usually free for wheelchair users and companions; call ahead or check with the tourist office. Specialist websites, such as www.europeforvisitors. com, list accessible hotels. The **Sage Travel** website is packed with detailed information. **Can Be Done** specializes in holidays and tailor-made packages.

Senior Travellers

Senior travellers are eligible for reduced fees to churches and museums, with a photographic ID as proof of age. If travelling by train, it's best to buy the *carta d'argento*, which gives over-60s a 15 percent discount. Yearly card costs €30 (free to over-75s) and is available at stations, travel agencies or online.

Students and Young People

Students should bring an **International Student Identity Card (ISIC)** card with them for reduced fares and entry fees. Those aged 14 to 29 can get a **Venezia Unica** card (€6) for a 72-hour pass (€22) on public transport and other discounts.

Travelling with Children

Family passes are available for the *vaporetti*, museums and churches. Children under 6 travel free on public transport, and discounted or free entry to sights come with the Chorus Pass (under 11) and Museum Pass (under 6; *see p143*). Most restaurants will have children's meals. Carry a pushchair, as negotiating the bridges can be tiring.

DIRECTORY

PASSPORTS AND VISAS

Australia
Via Borgogna 2, Milan
📞 02 7767 4200
🌐 italy.embassy.gov.au

Canada
Via Zara 30, Rome
📞 06 854 442 911 (24hrs)
🌐 canadainternational.
gc.ca

Italian Foreign Office
🌐 esteri.it

New Zealand
Via Terraggio 17, Milan
📞 02 721 70001
🌐 nzembassy.com/italy

UK
Via San Paolo 7, Milan
📞 02 723 001 (24 hrs)
🌐 gov.uk/government/
world/italy

US
Via Principe Amadeo
2/10, Milan
📞 02 290 351
🌐 milan.usconsulate.gov

CUSTOMS AND IMMIGRATION

Customs Information
🌐 visahq.com

TRAVEL SAFETY ADVICE

Australia
Australian Department of Foreign Affairs and Trade
🌐 dfat.gov.au
🌐 smartraveller.gov.au

United Kingdom
UK Foreign and Commonwealth Office
🌐 gov.uk/foreign-
travel-advice

United States
US Department of State
🌐 travel.state.gov

HEALTH

Health Venice
🌐 healthvenice.com

Ospedale SS Giovanni e Paolo
MAP F3 ■ Castello 6777
📞 118 (for emergencies)

PERSONAL SECURITY

ACTV Lost Property
MAP B3 ■ Garage Communale, Piazzale Roma
📞 041 272 21 79

City Lost Property
MAP P4 ■ Ca' Farsetti, San Marco 4136
📞 041 274 82 25

Questura
MAP B3 ■ Fondamente di S Chiara, Santa Croce, 500
📞 041 271 55 86

TRAVELLERS WITH SPECIFIC NEEDS

Can Be Done
🌐 canbedone.co.uk

Sage Travel
🌐 sagetraveling.com

Sanitrans
📞 041 523 99 77
🌐 sanitrans.net

STUDENTS AND YOUNG PEOPLE

International Student Identity Card
🌐 isic.org

Venezia Unica
🌐 veneziaunica.it

Currency and Banking

Italy uses the euro, the common currency of the European Union. Bank notes come in seven denominations – 5, 10, 20, 50, 100, 200 and 500 – and coins, eight: 1, 2, 5, 10, 20 and 50 cents, plus €1 and €2. There is no limit on the amount of cash you can bring into the country.

Banks are usually open 8:30am—1:30pm Monday to Friday and close at weekends and public holidays. Almost all banks have a cashpoint or ATM (bancomat), which displays the logos of the cards they accept, as well as giving multilingual instructions. Be careful to shield your PIN, which should consist of four digits only. It's worth checking whether you need to inform your bank that you will be making foreign withdrawals before you leave. You should also find out the rate of commission and transaction charges. All major credit and debit cards (Mastercard, Visa, American Express) are widely accepted in Italy's hotels, restaurants and shops. If you lose a card or have it stolen, report it immediately on the appropriate emergency number from your provider.

Foreign-exchange offices are open seven days a week, but commission rates tend to be high. Those at Venice's train station and airport stay open until the evening and at weekends. Post offices offer the same service.

Telephone and Internet

Tri-band and GSM mobile phones will work in Italy, but confirm the roaming charges before you leave. The alternative – if your mobile can be unlocked – is to buy an Italian pay-as-you-go SIM card from **TIM**, **Wind** or **Vodafone**. Top-ups are available from tobacconists (tabacchi) and newsstands, where you can also buy phonecards (carte telefoniche) for public phone boxes. When calling an Italian landline, it must be prefixed by its full area code even within the city you are calling from, and the 0 must be kept when dialling an Italian number from abroad. To call Venice from abroad, dial the access code 00 39 (0 11 39 from the US and Canada, 00 11 39 from Australia), followed by the 041 city code. Mobile numbers begin with 3 and are not prefixed by a 0. Skype (www.skype.com) is the cheapest option for international calls.

Internet and Wi-Fi is widely available in hotels, some restaurants and cafés. You can buy access to the municipal Venice Wi-Fi network for 24hrs, 72hrs or a week through the Venezia Unica card, though this focuses on the main squares and thoroughfares.

Postal Services

Stamps (francobolli) can be bought at post offices and tabacchi, which are recognizable by the black-and-white "T" sign. Post offices are open in the morning Monday to Saturday. You can find a complete list with opening hours on the **Italian Post** website. Use the Posta Prioritaria service if you want letters to arrive quickly.

Television and Radio

Beside the three state TV channels – RAI 1, RAI 2 and RAI 3 – satellite and cable TV transmit foreign channels such as CNN, Sky News, and the BBC World Service in many languages. The main radio stations – Radio 1, Radio 2 and Radio 3 – are also run by RAI. Venice Classic Radio (www.veniceclassic radio.com) and La Fenice Radio (www.lafenice. radio.net) both stream Italian classical music.

Newspapers

European and US newspapers are sold at large newsagents a day or so after publication. Local daily newspapers such as Il Gazzettino and La Nuova Venezia are useful for event listings, as is the national daily Corriere della Sera.

Opening Hours

Many museums are open daily, but times are subject to change, so it is wise to check. The main churches are usually open 10am–5pm Monday to Saturday. Food shops are open 9am–1pm and 4–7.30pm Monday to Saturday, except for Wednesday afternoon. In low season, clothing and gift stores close all day Sunday and also Monday mornings.

Public Holidays

Venice observes the following public holidays: New Year's Day (1 Jan), Epiphany (6 Jan), Easter Monday (variable), Liberation Day and St Mark's Day (both celebrated on 25 Apr) Labour Day (1 May), Republic Day (2 Jun), Assumption (15 Aug), All Saints' Day (1 Nov), Salute (21 Nov), Immaculate Conception (8 Dec), Christmas Day (25 Dec), Boxing Day (26 Dec).

Time Difference

Italy is one hour ahead of Greenwich Mean Time (GMT) and changes to Daylight Saving Time (ora legale) from the Last Sunday in March to the last Sunday in October, putting the country two hours ahead of GMT. For all official purposes, Italy uses the 24-hour clock.

Electrical Appliances

The electrical current in Italy is 220V AC with two-pin, round-pronged plugs. Bring a travel adapter for electrical appliances.

Weather

Every season in Venice has its attractions, but July and August can get very hot (up to 30° C/ 86° F) and sticky. Spring and autumn are cooler (around 15° C/59° F). Between October and March, Venice often experiences acqua alta (tidal flooding), which spreads out from Piazza San Marco. Sirens give an alert to an impending flood, and a network of passerelle (wooden walkways) are erected on the main routes around the city. You can buy plastic overshoes and find details on tide height on the comune.venezia website.

Visitor Information

There are official tourist offices, Informazioni Turistiche, (IAT) at the airport, in Piazza San Marco, Santa Lucia train station and at Piazzale Roma, which provide city and vaporetto maps and other information. The free monthly magazine Un Ospite di Venezia – published in English as A Guest in Venice – gives listings, useful practical information, and boat timetables and is widely distributed in hotels. Look out, too, for wall posters advertising local festivities and cultural events. You can also pick up details of what's on from the tourist offices, or consult the websites in the directory on this page. If you intend visiting a number of churches, consider a Chorus Pass (€12), which gives entry to 18 churches and organizes guided tours. (Single entrance to churches costs €3.) Though you are not required to cover your head, it is important to dress respectfully when visiting churches and avoid bare arms, shorts and beachwear. The Museum Pass (€24) allows entry to 11 museums. The most comprehensive pass, however, is the Venezia Unica city pass (see p141), which you can tailor to your needs. It gives access to museums, churches, vaporetti, public toilets and Wi-Fi. It is also available at various points around the city and online.

DIRECTORY

TELEPHONE SERVICES

TIM
☎ 041 521 04 83
🌐 tim.it

Vodafone
☎ 041 296 01 43
🌐 vodafone.it

Wind
☎ 049 261 06 54
🌐 wind.it

POSTAL SERVICES

Italian Post
🌐 poste.it

Main Post Office
MAP P3 ■ Calle Larga de L'Ascension, San Marco 1241

WEATHER

🌐 ilmeteo.it

Tide Height Information
🌐 comune.venezia.it/ maree

VISITOR INFORMATION

IAT
☎ 041 2424
🌐 veneziaunica.it

Un Ospite di Venezia
🌐 unospitedivenezia.it

Chorus Pass
☎ 041 275 04 62
🌐 chorusvenezia.org

Museum Pass
🌐 visitmuve.it

USEFUL WEBSITES

🌐 labiennale.org
🌐 venezia.net
🌐 venezia.travel
🌐 veneziaunica.it
🌐 veniceforyou.com
🌐 visit-venice-italy.com

Trips and Tours

The official tour guides, **Cooperativa Guide Turistiche Autorizzate,** give you in-depth history for every corner of Venice in 15 different languages. Tours with English-speaking guides can be booked through tourist offices and agencies such as **A Guide in Venice** and **Bucintoro Viaggi**, which also organizes gondola rides, working out more affordably if you are part of a group.

You can learn to row like a gondolier with qualified English-speaking instructors with **Row Venice**. Prices start at €85 per person.

Private tours of some of Venice's museums can be combined with historical walking tours through **Venice Museums,** and the **Jewish Museum** offers a guided tour of three of the synagogues in the Ghetto Nuovo (see p103). They can also arrange tours of the old Jewish cemetery on the Lido (see p123).

Outside of Venice, you can spend a full day or half a day cruising the Brenta Canal on the motorboat **Il Burchiello**, which includes visiting the Palladian villas, once the summer residences of Venetian nobility. The return journey from Padua is made by bus.

Shopping

Venice has myriad fascinating shops, a selection of which has been picked out for inclusion in each district in this book. Glass and beads, masks, handmade paper and paper goods, lace and gondolier hats are all popular souvenir items with tourists.

When buying glassware, it is worth shopping around: many glass shops stock similar items, and prices can vary wildly. Murano tends to be more expensive than Venice, but you get a free demonstration as well. Make sure you can see the authentic Vetro Artistico® Murano trademark before buying anything that is claimed to be from Murano. Virtually all glass-shop staff are experts in packaging fragile and bulky items, and they can arrange for forwarding overseas by air or sea. Always check that insurance is included. Visitors from non-EU countries can claim a tax refund on purchases that exceed €155 from one shop. Most shopkeepers will have the appropriate forms.

The Mercerie – the district that joins the Rialto Bridge to Piazza San Marco – has a concentration of high-end stores such as Dolce & Gabbana, Prada and Armani selling designer clothing, shoes and handbags. Calle Larga XXII Marzo also has a cluster of chic shops. In the Cannaregio district, **T Fondaco dei Tedeschi**, the only department store in Venice, stock upmarket designer brands and are open every day of the week.

Delicatessen, bakeries and specialist shops are centred around the Rialto Market, where you can find enticing displays of fresh produce. For food shopping, there are a number of supermarkets throughout the city – Coop Adriatica, Conad and Punto, for instance – which stay open late and on Sundays. Note that shopkeepers are obliged by law to give you a receipt. Street sellers do a brisk trade in tourist bric-à-brac, as well as imitation designer bags and accessories. However, be warned that hefty fines are imposed for anyone who is caught buying counterfeit goods.

Dining

Restaurant opening hours are generally 12:30–2:30pm and 7–10pm. Venice caters mainly to tourists, often on a day trip, so the further you venture from the main tourist spots, the less likely you are to find a menu turistico and waiters luring you in, and the more likely you are to discover good Venetian cuisine. It's best to book ahead as restaurants are often small. The cover charge (coperto) of around €2 and a service charge (servizio) of up to 12 per cent should be indicated clearly on the menu and also on the bill.

Venetians often take an early evening giro all'ombra (stroll in the shade), which involves eating cicheti (snacks) with wine, in various local bacari (small bars). The classic Venetian aperitivo is a spritz – a mixture of white wine, Aperol and sparkling mineral water.

Because the city is situated between a lagoon and the sea, plenty of fish appears on restaurant menus – Venetian specialities include baby cuttlefish cooked in its own ink and eel cooked in Marsala wine. Look out for traditional *bigoli* (a long thick, dark pasta), *frittelle alla Veneziana* (fried sweet doughnuts with lemon and Marsala) and the almond confectionery *torrone*. Burano residents are proud of their *bussolai* (ring-shaped cinnamon-flavoured biscuits). Italians never drink a cappuccino after lunch or dinner, instead choosing an espresso or a *digestivo*.

Pizza places are less expensive than restaurants, as is the self-service Brek chain. For something more substantial, find a *tavola calda* (cafeteria), where hot meals are served at a counter. Vegetarian restaurants are a rarity – Le Spighe in Castello is one *(see p113)* – but you can find vegetarian choices at many restaurants.

Drinking coffee in bars while standing up, as the locals do, will cost you half as much as sitting at a table. The ultimate, albeit ultra-expensive, coffee experience is sitting at either Caffè Florian or Quadri's in "Europe's drawing room" of Piazza San Marco *(see pp20–21)*, while an orchestra plays and you simply watch the world go by.

Note that smoking is prohibited in bars, restaurants and all public indoor places, though electronic cigarettes are permitted. Picnicking on bridges, church steps or in Piazza San Marco incurs a steep fine (€150). Look for a bench in one of the squares or parks instead, and eat discreetly, or find an authorised picnic area. For picnic areas see **#EnjoyRespectVenezia**.

Accommodation

Venice's hotels cater for every budget, although being mainly small (20 rooms or fewer), they book up quickly. It's wise to book as far ahead as you can and to look for special deals online. Spaces fill up quickly at Carnival time in February or early March, as well as for the Film Festival in September. The Venice Biennale is held in odd-numbered years and also puts an extra strain on accommodation.

Hotels nearest Piazza San Marco are the most expensive, and a view of a canal costs more. The Lido and mainland Mestre are less expensive but can be noisier, since they are not traffic-free. Northern Cannaregio and eastern Castello are quiet areas; Dorsoduro has more bars and nightlife. There is also a good choice of guesthouses, bed and breakfasts, hostels and even camping sites. Apartments and house exchanges are another possibility to consider.

Travel for Kids has an extensive list of apartments and hotels that are suitable for families.

Truly Venice offers luxury apartments, with plenty for larger groups.

Prices are by room, so check whether breakfast is included. Hotel prices are generally low between early November and Easter and high during the Carnival period from February to March. Some hotels are also cheaper in July and August, when the city can get very humid. When booking, keep in mind that you will have to walk from the *vaporetto* stop and the amount of luggage you will be carrying; it's best kept to a minimum, since porters are expensive. Cases on wheels should be carried over bridges to limit damage to the pavements and reduce noise pollution.

DIRECTORY

Places to Stay

PRICE CATEGORIES

For a standard, double room per night (with breakfast if included), taxes and extra charges.

€ under €150   €€ €150–350   €€€ over €350

Luxury Hotels

Grand Hotel Palazzo dei Dogi

MAP D1 ■ Fondamenta Madonna dell'Orto, Cannaregio 35 00 ■ 041 220 81 11 ■ www.dahotels.com ■ €€
On a quiet Cannaregio canal, with a lovely garden stretching back to the lagoon, this former convent is furnished with Murano chandeliers and fabrics crafted by leading artisans. This is the best-value luxury hotel in town, and has its own guest launch.

Aman Venice

MAP N3 ■ San Polo 1364 ■ 041 270 73 33 ■ www.aman.com ■ €€€
The hotel launch brings guests from the airport to the Grand Canal entrance of Palazzo Papadopoli. You step straight into the original palace, with its stuccoed rooms, as well as a small spa and a gym. The hotel also has spacious common rooms and lovely gardens.

Bauer Palazzo

MAP P5 ■ Campo San Moisè, S Marco 1459 ■ 041 520 70 22 ■ www.bauerhotels.com ■ €€€
Close to St Mark's Square amid the main sights and the best shops, the majestic Bauer offers old-style service in elegant surroundings.

Excelsior Venice Lido Resort

MAP H2 ■ Lungomare Marconi 41, Lido ■ 041 526 02 01 ■ www.hotelexcelsiorvenezia.com ■ Closed Nov–mid-Mar ■ €€€
Crawling with stars during the Film Festival, this hotel has rooms right on the beach. There is also a swimming pool and exclusive restaurants.

Hotel Cipriani

MAP E6 ■ Giudecca 10 ■ 041 520 77 44 ■ www.hotelcipriani.com ■ Closed Nov–Mar ■ €€€
Set on Giudecca, Cipriani is just minutes from the water. It has a private garden with a salt-water pool, and three top restaurants (see p64).

Hotel Danieli

MAP R5 ■ Riva degli Schiavoni, Castello 4196 ■ 041 522 64 80 ■ www.danielihotelvenice.com ■ €€€
Set in a pink palazzo, Danieli has a long history of famous guests (see p109). The hotel is close to the Bridge of Sighs and Piazza San Marco.

JW Marriott Venice Resort

MAP N4 ■ Isole delle Rose, Venice Lagoon ■ 041 852 13 00 ■ www.jwvenice.com ■ Closed Nov–Feb ■ €€€
In parkland on an island in the Southern Lagoon, this resort offers suites, roof terraces, swimming pools, a spa and a choice of restaurants, as well as daily cooking classes. The private shuttle launch takes 20 minutes to reach Piazza San Marco.

Luna Hotel Baglioni

MAP P5 ■ Calle Larga dell'Ascension, S Marco 1243 ■ 041 528 98 40 ■ www.baglionihotels.com ■ €€€
Enjoy exquisite service in a refined atmosphere of chandeliers and marble. This is Venice's oldest hotel – it hosted the Knights Templar in the 1100s, while they waited to embark for the Crusades. Breakfast is served in the drawing room, frescoed by pupils of Tiepolo (see p48).

Metropole

MAP F4 ■ Riva degli Schiavoni, Castello 4149 ■ 041 520 50 44 ■ www.hotelmetropole.com ■ €€€
This grand good-value establishment is immaculately run. On the waterfront, minutes from San Marco, it boasts a wonderful garden and a Michelin-starred restaurant.

Palace Bonvecchiati

MAP Q4 ■ Calle dei Fabbri, S Marco 4680 ■ 041 296 31 11 ■ www.palacebonvecchiati.it ■ €€€
"Contemporary luxury" best describes this hotel with a roof-level sauna and gym. Private canal access means guests can arrive by water taxi.

St Regis Europa & Regina

MAP P6 ■ Corte Barozzi, S Marco 2159 ■ 041 240 00 01 ■ www.westin europareginavenice.com ■ €€€

This elegant historic palace, on the Grand Canal, is beautifully decorated. It is also quite close to the Piazza San Marco.

Budget Hotels

Al Campaniel Guesthouse

MAP L4 ■ Calle del Campaniel, S Polo 2889 ■ 041 275 07 49 ■ al campaniel.tripod.com ■ €

Spanish-Venetian couple Gloria and Marco are discreet and professional hosts offering spotless rooms close to the San Tomà boat stop. Each room has tea- and coffee-making facilities.

Alloggi Gerotto Calderan

MAP C2 ■ Campo S Geremia, Cannaregio 283 ■ 041 715 361 ■ Closed Christmas week ■ www.casagerottocalderan.com ■ No credit cards ■ €

Handy for the station, this hotel has airy rooms, some with bath (no breakfast). Guests are welcomed by enthusiastic English-speaking staff. Try to bargain down the rates in low season.

Al Santo

Via del Santo 147, Padua ■ 049 875 21 31 ■ Closed 7–30 Jan ■ www.alsanto.it ■ €

This simple family-run hotel is very well located, 10 minutes' stroll from Padua's main historic sights (see p129).

Bernardi Semenzato

MAP P1 ■ Calle dell'Oca, Cannaregio 4366 ■ 041 522 72 57 ■ www.hotel bernardi.com ■ €

Located near Campo dei Santi Apostoli, this hotel is a delightful bargain. The owners are extremely hospitable.

Casa Cardinal Piazza

MAP D1 ■ Fondamenta Contarini, Cannaregio 3539/A ■ 041 721 388 ■ www.casacardinal piazza.org ■ No credit cards ■ No air conditioning ■ €

Run by friendly nuns, this great-value palace guest-house is set in a shady garden right on the lagoon edge. It has 24 modest rooms with bathrooms. Breakfast is available; there's an 11pm curfew.

Hotel Gobbo

MAP C2 ■ Campo S Geremia 312, Cannaregio ■ 041 715 001 ■ www. albergoalgobbo.it ■ €

The "Hunchback" is a clean, small-scale hotel. Most of the rooms have air conditioning, and a couple overlook a bustling square. Easy access from the railway station.

Istituto Canossiano

MAP K6 ■ Fondamenta delle Eremite, Dorsoduro 1323 ■ 041 240 97 11 ■ Closed Christmas week, 2 weeks in Aug ■ www. romite1323.com ■ No air conditioning ■ €

This modernized, converted convent has vast courtyards to wander around. Vending machines are on hand for snacks and drinks; otherwise, it's not far to the Zattere. Guests should note that there's a midnight curfew.

Il Lato Azzurro

MAP H2 ■ Via Forti 13, Sant'Erasmo ■ 041 523 06 42 ■ www.latoazzurro.it ■ No air conditioning ■ €

Il Lato Azzurro offers great-value lodgings on this garden island, where sea breezes are ensured. The hosts can arrange canoe trips, use of bicycles, picnic lunches and half-board, consisting mainly of vegetarian meals. The hotel has two rooms specially equipped for travellers with specific needs.

San Giorgio Monastery

MAP F5 ■ Isola di San Giorgio Maggiore ■ 041 241 47 17 ■ No credit cards ■ €

The monks on San Giorgio Island, just across the Canale di San Marco from Piazza San Marco, welcome guests to their peaceful premises. A simple breakfast is provided, and self-catering accommodation is also available. There are superb views of Venice from the square in front of the church.

Hotels with Charm

B&B Ca' Noemi

MAP F1 ■ Rio Terà 32, Malamocco ■ 041 242 00 40 ■ www.canoemi.it ■ €

This recently renovated 14th-century building is located on the southern end of the Lido in an old fishing village. The nearby Ca 'del Moro Sporting Club has a swimming pool, tennis and physical fitness facilities. There is easy access to the city and the beach.

Accademia Villa Maravege

MAP L6 ■ Fondamenta Bollani, Dorsoduro 1058 ■ 041 521 01 88 ■ www.pensioneaccademia.it ■ €€–€€€

This beautiful 17th-century villa near the Accademia (see pp30–31) was formerly the Russian embassy. Breakfast can be enjoyed in the private garden. You need to book well in advance.

Ca' della Corte

MAP B3 ■ Corte Surian, Dorsoduro 3560 ■ 041 715 877 ■ www.cadellacorte.com ■ €€

This charming bed-and-breakfast has spotless rooms that boast all the latest equipment, including satellite TV. It is just a short stroll to Piazzale Roma.

La Calcina

MAP D5 ■ Zattere, Dorsoduro 780 ■ 041 520 64 66 ■ www.lacalcina.com ■ €€

In 1877, Ruskin stayed at this guesthouse on the Zattere. The rooms have been modernized since then, but they retain their charm and parquet floors. An exclusive street-level terrace overlooks the Giudecca Canal, while another surveys the rooftops. It is advised to book well in advance for a stay here.

Hotel Flora

MAP P5 ■ Calle Bergamaschi, S Marco 2283/A ■ 041 520 58 44 ■ www.hotelflora.it ■ €€

Though small, the pretty internal courtyard with lush greenery at this 17th-century palazzo is an oasis of calm after the city crowds. The charming rooms are individually decorated. Those on the upper floor offer good views.

Hotel Marconi

MAP P3 ■ Riva del Vin, S Polo 729 ■ 041 522 20 68 ■ www.hotelmarconi.it ■ €€

This popular hotel by Rialto Bridge has outside seating reserved for guests. Rooms are simple but guests are given a warm welcome.

Locanda Cipriani

MAP H1 ■ Piazza S Fosca 29, Torcello ■ 041 730 150 ■ www.locandacipriani.com ■ Closed Jan–early Feb ■ €€

A peaceful, sophisticated hotel on the island of Torcello (see pp36–7), Locanda Cipriani has a list of illustrious past guests, and a famed restaurant overlooking the garden. Guests can explore the island after the day-trippers have left.

Palazzo Abadessa

MAP D2 ■ Calle Priuli, Cannaregio 4011 ■ 041 241 37 84 ■ www.abadessa.com ■ €€–€€€

Murano glass chandeliers and lovely fabrics add to the authentic atmosphere at this palace hotel. There are two specially equipped rooms for travellers with specific needs.

San Simon Ai Due Fanali

MAP K1 ■ Campo S Simeone Grande, S Croce 946/949 ■ 041 718 490 ■ www.aiduefanali.com ■ €€

The rooms at this tastefully renovated former monastery have wooden rafters. Several apartments are available near the Arsenale.

The Gritti Palace

MAP N6 ■ Campo S Maria del Giglio, S Marco 2467 ■ 041 794 611 ■ www.thegrittipalace.com ■ €€€

Ernest Hemingway stayed in this 15th-century palace-hotel situated on the Grand Canal. Romantic waterside dining is among its many features.

Converted Palaces

Albergo Guerrato

MAP N2 ■ Calle Drio la Scimia, S Polo 240/A ■ 041 522 71 31 ■ Closed 7–30 Jan ■ www.hotelguerrato.it ■ Not all rooms are en suite ■ €

This charming, spacious old hotel at Rialto dates back to 1288 and is full of history.

Al Sole

MAP J4 ■ Fondamenta Minotto, S Croce 136 ■ 041 244 03 28 ■ www.alsolehotels.com ■ €€

A beautiful place to stay, convenient for Piazzale Roma, this 16th-century palace, with a huge lobby and a courtyard draped in wisteria, is often used as a film set. Rooms have all mod cons.

Ca' Nigra Lagoon Resort

MAP K1 ■ Campo S Simeon Grande, S Croce 927 ■ 041 524 27 90 ■ www.hotelcanigra.com ■ €€–€€€

Once an ambassador's residence, this palace on the Grand Canal has two delightful shady gardens. The decor is modern, and one room even has a private jacuzzi. The location is handy for the railway and bus stations.

Ca' Pisani

MAP F4 ■ Rio Terrà Foscarini, Dorsoduro 979A ■ 041 240 14 11 ■ www.capisanihotel.it ■ €€

Converted in 2000, Ca' Pisani has a warm ambience, stunning modern design and all the facilities you could hope for. You may never want to leave this 15th-century palace, conveniently close to the Accademia.

Hotel Santo Stefano

MAP M5 ■ Campo S Stefano, S Marco 2957 ■ 041 520 01 66 ■ www.hotelsantostefano venezia.com ■ €€

Guests return to this former monastery watchtower for its discerning style, maximum comfort (there are Jacuzzis in all the rooms) and breathtaking views.

Locanda La Corte

MAP F3 ■ Calle Bressana, Castello 6317 ■ 041 241 13 00 ■ www.locanda lacorte.it ■ €€

A relaxing atmosphere prevails at this renovated 16th-century palace. It once served the ambassador from Brescia and is impeccably furnished with period pieces. Breakfast is served in the courtyard.

Locanda San Barnaba

MAP L5 ■ Calle del Traghetto, Dorsoduro 2785–2786 ■ 041 241 12 33 ■ www.locanda-san barnaba.com ■ €€

Minutes from the Ca' Rezzonico ferry stop, this quiet, elegant

palace-hotel has original frescoes in many of the rooms, which are named after Goldoni's plays.

San Cassiano – Ca' Favretto

MAP N2 ■ Calle della Rosa, S Croce 2232 ■ 041 524 17 68 ■ www.san cassiano.it ■ €€

Right on the Grand Canal, but hidden away in the maze of alleyways close to Rialto, you'll find this 16th-century palace which has been converted into a hotel named after a 19th-century artist. It offers elegant, well-equipped rooms with Venetian furnishings.

Ruzzini Palace Hotel

MAP R3 ■ Campo S Maria Formosa, Castello 5866 ■ 041 241 04 47 ■ www.ruzzinipalace.com ■ €€€

Constructed in the late 16th century, this period residence retains its vast frescoed rooms, monumental staircases and a water entrance. It overlooks a typical Venetian square and is only five minutes from Piazza San Marco.

Hotels in Tranquil Locations

Agriturismo Le Garzette

MAP H2 ■ Lungomare Alberoni 32, Malamocco, Lido ■ 041 731 078 ■ Closed Christmas–Feb ■ www.legarzette.it ■ €

This attractive family-run establishment, off the beaten track, has only five rooms and this – along with the superb home cooking – will make you feel as though you are part

of the family. It is located very close to the sea and the lagoon.

Ca' San Marcuola

MAP C2 ■ Campiello della Chiesa, Cannaregio 1763 ■ 041 716 048 ■ Closed Dec–Carnival ■ www. casanmarcuola.com ■ €

In a handy location close to the *vaporetto* stop, this unpretentious, but quiet and friendly, guesthouse is well appointed.

Due Mori

Contrà Do Rode 24–26, Vicenza ■ 044 432 18 86 ■ Closed 1–15 Aug ■ www.hotelduemori.com ■ No air conditioning ■ €

In a quiet street in Vicenza, close to all the main sights *(see p130)*, the Due Mori has spacious, spotless rooms furnished in old-style dark timber.

Villa Ducale

Riviera Martiri della Libertà 75, Dolo ■ ACTV bus 53 from Piazzale Roma ■ 041 560 80 20 ■ www.villaducale.it ■ €

Halfway between Padua and Venice, this stately residence stands in a lovely private park with statues. The beautiful rooms have the usual facilities plus frescoes and glass chandeliers.

Ca' Vendramin di Santa Fosca

MAP D2 ■ Fondamenta Vendramin, Cannaregio 2400 ■ 041 275 01 25 ■ www.hotelcaven dramin.it ■ €€

The comfortable rooms in this cosy 16th-century palazzo just off the Strada Nova are lavishly decorated. Breakfast is served in a period-style room with stained-glass windows.

For a key to hotel price categories see p146

Dell'Alboro

MAP M4 ▪ Corte dell'Alboro, S Marco 3894/A-B ▪ 041 522 94 54 ▪ Closed 20 Nov–20 Dec ▪ www.alborohotel.it ▪ €€

Located in a relaxing residential area near the Sant'Angelo boat stop, this hotel has rooms with all modern facilities and is centrally located for Piazza San Marco.

Hotel Falier

MAP K4 ▪ Salizzada S Pantalon, S Croce 130 ▪ 041 710 882 ▪ www. hotelfalier.com ▪ €€

This cheery hotel is named after the beheaded traitor Doge Falier, "as a warning to guests who fail to pay!" Sunlight streams into the comfortable, if small, rooms, all of which have an ensuite shower. There's a courtyard dripping with wisteria.

Locanda Fiorita

MAP M5 ▪ Campiello Novo o dei Morti, S Marco 3457/A ▪ 041 523 47 54 ▪ www.locandafiorita.com ▪ €€

The very pretty Locanda Fiorita is located on a sunny square that was once a public cemetery off Campo San Stefano. In spring and summer, enjoy a leisurely breakfast out-side. Bargain for cheaper rooms in low season.

Bauer Palladio

MAP E6 ▪ Giudecca 33 ▪ 041 520 70 22 ▪ Closed mid-Nov–Mar ▪ www. palladiohotelspa.com ▪ €€€

This exclusive spa hotel was originally designed in the 1500s by Palladio as an orphanage. It has an array of facilities,

including a spa and fitness centre, a vast garden and a restaurant.

Medium-Priced Hotels

Al Gallion

MAP K2 ▪ Calle Gallion, S Croce 1126 ▪ 348 814 15 76 ▪ www.algallion. com ▪ No credit cards ▪ No air conditioning ▪ €

Guests are given a warm welcome and insider infor-mation at this small B&B. It is handy for Piazzale Roma and the Riva di Biasio *vaporetto* stop on the Grand Canal.

Al Saor

MAP P1 ▪ Calle Zotti, Cannaregio 3904/A ▪ 041 296 06 54 ▪ www.alsaor.com ▪ €

The owners of this family-run establishment, close to the Ca' d'Oro, offer personal touches: a ride in their own boat for guests, and home-made biscuits for breakfast.

Hotel Torcolo

Vicolo Listone 3, Verona ▪ Bus Nos. 11, 12, 13, 51 (or 90, 92, 93 evenings & hols) from Marciapiede A ▪ 045 800 75 12 ▪ Closed Christmas week ▪ www. hoteltorcolo.it ▪ €

Just around the corner from the Arena, this hotel is run by a very friendly team. Guest parking is available.

Locanda Ca' Zose

MAP D5 ▪ Calle del Bastion, Dorsoduro 193/B ▪ 041 522 66 35 ▪ www. hotelcazose.com ▪ €–€€

Rooms are cosy and stylish in this 17th-century building; several have canal views. The hotel is in a very quiet location,

handy for La Salute *vaporetto* and the Peggy Guggenheim Collection.

Rossi

MAP C2 ▪ Calle Procuratie, Cannaregio 262 ▪ 041 715 562 ▪ Closed 6 Jan–6 Feb ▪ www.hotelrossivenice. com ▪ €

This popular family-friendly hotel is high on hospitality. Rooms are spotless, and many have lovely views. The hotel is well placed for Strada Nova. Book in advance.

Villa Giustinian

Via Miranese 85, Mirano ▪ 041 570 02 00 ▪ www. villagiustinian.com ▪ €

Housed in an 18th-century villa, this hotel has a swimming pool, park, magnificent rooms and a fine restaurant. Buses run every 20 minutes for the 40-minute trip to Venice.

Al Gambero

MAP P4 ▪ Calle dei Fabbri, S Marco 4687 ▪ 041 522 43 84 ▪ www.locanda algambero.com ▪ €€

This old favourite on a bridge halfway between the Rialto and Piazza San Marco is wonderfully located for many sights and shopping sprees. Downstairs is Le Bistrot de Venise, a popular nightspot (see p69).

Al Gazzettino

MAP Q4 ▪ Calle di Mezzo, S Marco 4971 ▪ 041 528 65 23 ▪ www.algazzettino. com ▪ €€

Centrally located between the Rialto and San Marco, Al Gazzettino is a basic, decent-value hotel. The downstairs walls are papered with sheets from the city's *Il Gazzettino* newspaper, which was its long-standing neighbour until its relocation to the more practical mainland.

Hotel Novecento
MAP N6 ▪ Calle del Dose, Campo San Maurizio, San Marco 2683 ▪ 041 241 37 65 ▪ www.nove cento.biz ▪ €€
The relaxing rooms at this boutique hotel, located halfway between the Accademia and Piazza San Marco, have Orientalist decor, with furniture and tapestries from the Far East. In summer, breakfast is served in the courtyard.

Hostels and Campsites

A&O Venezia Mestre
Via Ca Marcello 19, ▪ 041 884 09 90 ▪ www. aohostels.com ▪ €
Located opposite the Ponte della Libertà, in Mestre, this A&O hostel is six minutes' walking distance from the Venezia-Mestre train station. It offers single, double and dorm rooms, complete with lockers.

Campeggio Miramare
Lungomare D. Alighierl 29, Punta Sabbione ▪ 041 966 150 ▪ Closed Nov–late Mar ▪ www. camping-miramare.it ▪ €
One of the many camping grounds at Punta Sabbioni on the seaside of Venice, Miramare is linked to the city by ferry (line LN). The camping village has huts and campsites and also offers a range of facilities, including a mini-market and a restaurant-bar.

Camping Fusina
Via Moranzani 93, Fusina ▪ 041 547 00 55 ▪ www. camping-fusina.com ▪ €
This popular three-star venue for campers and backpackers (in a caravan) is right on the lagoon edge. It is well connected via bus No. 11 from Mestre train station or the Alilaguna ferry from the Zattere in Venice.

Foresteria Valdese
MAP R3 ▪ Calle Lunga S Maria Formosa, Castello 5170 ▪ 041 528 67 97 ▪ www.foresteria venezia.it ▪ €
A wonderful guesthouse near Campo Santa Maria Formosa (see p110), Foresteria Valdese is run by the Waldensian and Methodist community and has frescoed dormitories, and two, three and four-bed rooms. Be sure to book in advance.

IYH Città di Padova
Via Aleardo Aleardi 30, Padua ▪ Bus Nos. 8, 12 or tram from Padua railway station to Prato della Valle ▪ 049 875 22 19 ▪ Closed 22 Dec–6 Jan ▪ www. ostellopadova.it ▪ €
A bit out of the way, but only a short walk to the main sights, this hostel benefits from a beautiful setting in an ornamental grassy square.

IYH Ostello Olimpico
Viale Giuriolo 7, Vicenza ▪ Bus Nos. 2, 5 or 7 from the railway station ▪ 0444 540 222 ▪ Closed early Nov–Feb ▪ www.ostello vicenza.com ▪ €
This cheery, helpful hostel is close to the main tourist office and Teatro Olimpico (see p131). Discounts apply at a neighbouring

bar and restaurant. Internet point and bike hire are available.

IYH Ostello Venezia
MAP E6 ▪ Fondamenta Zitelle 86, Giudecca ▪ 041 877 82 88 ▪ www. generatorhostels.com ▪ €
This well-run hostel offers inexpensive meals and a lovely setting on Giudecca. It is a 35-minute trip by *vaporetto* from the railway station and 5 minutes by *vaporetto* to Piazza San Marco (see pp20–23).

IYH Ostello Villa Francescatti
Salita Fontana del Ferro 15, Verona ▪ Bus No. 73 (Mon–Sat), 91 (evenings & Sun) from the railway station ▪ 045 590 360 ▪ www.ostelloverona.it ▪ €
This 16th-century villa on the hillside above the Roman amphitheatre is a youth hostel with dormitories. It is 3 km (2 miles) from Verona's train station.

Ostello Santa Fosca
MAP D2 ▪ Fondamenta Canal, Cannaregio 2372 ▪ 041 715 775 ▪ www. ostellosantafosca.it ▪ €
Set in rambling convent grounds, this university student hostel lets out dorm beds to backpackers. Cooking facilities are available in summer.

Venezia Camping Village
MAP G1 ▪ Via Orlanda 8d, Mestre ▪ 041 531 28 28 ▪ Closed early Jan & Feb ▪ www.veneziavillage.it ▪ €
With immaculate buildings around and a pool, this site is popular for campers and bungalow rentals. Bus Nos. 5 and 19 take you to Venice in 10 minutes.

For a key to hotel price categories see p146

Index

Acknowledgments

Author

Gillian Price was born in England in 1953 and grew up in Sydney, Australia. She moved to Venice in 1981 and has written nine books on walking in Italy. Gillian has been contributing to DK's Eyewitness Guides since 1998.

Additional contributor Kate Hughes

Publishing Director Georgina Dee

Publisher Vivien Antwi

Design Director Phil Ormerod

Editorial Parnika Bagla, Michelle Crane, Rebecca Flynn, Rachel Fox, Freddie Marriage, Fíodhna Ní Ghríofa, Scarlett O'Hara, Adrian Potts, Sally Schafer, Sands Publishing Solutions

Cover Design Maxine Pedliham, Vinita Venugopal

Design Richard Czapnik, Sunita Gahir, Bharti Karakoti

Picture Research Susie Peachey, Ellen Root, Lucy Sienkowska, Oran Tarjan

Cartography Zafar ul Islam Khan, Suresh Kumar, Casper Morris

DTP Jason Little, George Nimmo, Azeem Siddiqui

Production Linda Dare

Factchecker Charles Hebbert

Proofreader Ruth Reisenberger

Indexer Helen Peters

Illustrator Chris Orr & Associates
First edition created by Book Creation Services Ltd, London

Commissioned Photography Demetrio Carrasco, John Heseltine, Anna Mockford, Roger Moss, William Reavell, Rough Guides/Michelle Grant, Rough Guides/James McConnachie, Rough Guides/Martin Richardson

Revisions Parnika Bagla, Federico Damonte, Bharti Karakoti, Sumita Khatwani, Shikha Kulkarni, Bandana Paul, Rada Radojicic, Pamela Santini, Rituraj Singh, Beverly Smart, Manjari Thakur

Picture Credits

The publisher would like to thank the following for their kind permission to reproduce their photographs:

Key: a-above; b-below/bottom; c-centre; f-far; l-left; r-right; t-top

4Corners: Luca Da Ros 4t.
Alamy Images: A.F. Archive 65tr; age fotostock/Jose Peral 61tl, 104crb; AGF Srl/Mark Edward Smith 14bl; Alessandro0770 15b; The Art Archive/Collection Dagli Orti 19tl, 23cl; Peter Barritt 27b, 32cla; Bildarchiv Monheim GmbH 36bl; blickwinkel 109br; Paul Carstairs 82c; Frank Chmura 86bl; dpa picture alliance 111bl; Eye Ubiquitous/Paul Seheult 37ca; Peter Erik Forsberg 75clb; F1online digitale Bildagentur GmbH 68t; funkyfood, London/Paul Williams 10cra; Rik Hamilton 6cla; Hemis.fr /Christian Guy 117bl; Heritage Image Partnership Ltd 55cl, / Fine Art Images 18tl; Peter Horree 54b; IML Image Group/Roberto Meazza 134bl; Interfoto 51bl, /Fine Arts 51tl; John Warburton-Lee Photography /Ken Scicluna 106clb; Rebecca Johnson 67bl; Konstantin Kalishko 23b; Roy Kaltschmidt 76b; John Keats 14cra; John Kellerman 17cra, 38–9, 104tl; Alvan

Kranzer 51tr; liszt collection/Quint & Lox 53bl; LOOK Die Bildagentur der Fotografen GmbH 12–3c; Dennis MacDonald 111cla; Martin Thomas Photography 114–5; Mary Evans Picture Library 50cb; Thomas Mayer 103tr; Moviestore Collection Ltd 53tr; Erick Nguyen 47bl; North Wind Picture Archives 50cla; Sergey Novikov 108ca; Chuck Pefley 35tl; peterforsberg 75cla; Ferdinando Piezzi 118tl; Prisma Archivo 52c; Prisma Bildagentur AG/Sonderegger Christof 59tl; Alex Ramsay 62t; Realy Easy Star/Giuseppe Masci 133bl; Reda & Co srl/Federico Meneghetti 129br; Matthias Scholz 55tr; TRAVELSCAPES 123tl; Unlisted Images, Inc./Fotosearch 38bl; Peter Vallance 59b; Martyn Vickery 34br; Visions of Serge L 119bl; Ross Warner 37tl, 61b; World History Archive 16cb, 54tl; Zoonar GmbH/Francesco Perre 39bc.
Arnoldo Battois: 84bc.
AWL Images: Jon Arnold 1.
Bacarando: 86c.
Osteria Bancogiro: 93ca.
Bevilacqua Tessuti: 85crb.
Bistrot de Venise: 67b.
Signor Blum: 100clb.
Bragorà: 112bl.
Bridgeman Images: Cameraphoto Arte Venezia 19b.
Cesare Sent SNC: 120tc.
Corbis: Alinari Archives/Mauro Magliani 31clb; Atlantide Phototravel/Stefano Amantini 63cr; David Lees 31cla; Sylvain Sonnet 17cl; The Gallery Collection 15cl.
Dorling Kindersley: John Heseltine 44tr, 44b, 45cl
Dreamstime.com: Andreykr 34–5; Antonella865 37bc; Michal Bednarek 24–5; Canonman29 25cra, 82tr, 89tr; Carolannefreeling 46clb; Marco Clarizia 33tr; Crisferra 58c; Dbdella 34clb; Razvan Ionut Dragomirescu 110cla; Viorel Dudau 52tl; Eg004713 128tl; Ekaterinabelova 18br; Emicristea 13tr; Fedecandoniphoto 25br; Inna Felker 47tr; Michael Foley 49tr; Gekkon4ik 26crb; Ihsan Gercelman 6br; Radu Razvan Gheorghe 75tr; Diana Gradeva 116cla; Mark Graham 11ca; Neil Harrison 13cr; Anna Hristova 88cra; Lukasz Janyst 20–21; Wieslaw Jarek 10cl, 20br, 21bl; Jocrebbin 118bl; Johnnydevil 11br; Krontus 112c; Lachris77 2tr, 42–3; Lejoch 17tl, 46t; Ron Lima 4b; Lornet 10bl; Lucidwaters 73tr; Mapics 10–11b; Milosk50 32–3, 39tl; minnystock 28tl, 8–9; Evgeniya Moroz 12–13; NatashaBreen 36–7; Nikonaft 123br; Andrey Omelyanchuk 43clb; Carlos Sanchez Pereyra 118crb; Phant 4cla; Valeriya Potapova 94–5; Rndmst 45tr; Sandyprints 77tr; Sborisov 24bl, 28–9; Jozef Sedmak 83bl, 99tl, 105cla; Sindorei 109r; Paula Stanley 74tl; Stevanzz 3tr, 7cl, 16c, 35b, 59cr, 136–7; Stokkete 101c; Christophe Testi 98ca; Rachel Thomas 112tr; Giovanni Triggiani 27cla; Christophe Villedieu 12clb; Niko Vukelic 3tl, 78–9; Tosca Weijers 130c; Oleg Znamenskiy 90bl, 96tl, 117cra.
Enoiteca Mascareta: 113cr.
Enoteca Do Colonne: 70br.
Fondazione Musei Civici di Venezia: Ca' Pesaro – Galleria Internazionale d'Arte Moderna «November» 1870 by Telemaco Signorini 57bl; Ca' Rezzonico – Museo del Settecento Veneziano Scalone d'onore, (1753–1756) by Giorgio Massari 24br; Museo Correr 57cla, Mark Edward Smith 22bl, statue of Orfeo (1775–1776) Pietra di Vicenza by

Antonio Canova photo Mark Edward Smith 22ca;
Museo Storico Navale 57cr; Museo del Vetro,
Murano Murano Glass, Compagnia Venezia Murano,
1878 56bc; Palazzo Ducale 16bl, 17c; Palazzo
Fortuny/Courtesy Galleria Traghetto Venezia
Shadows by Anne-Karin Furunes photo by Mark
Edward Smith 83cla.
Fondazione Teatro La Fenice: MIchera Crosera 64tl,
64bl, 81br.
Getty Images: Awakening 65clb; DEA/Dagli Orti
52bc, /F. Ferruzzi 11tl; DeAgostini 30–31, 33cr, 36cl;
Fine Art Images /Heritage Images 30clb; Picture
Pos /Kurt Hutton 53cla; Mats Silvan 25tl.
Harry's Dolci: 127cra.
L'Isola – Carlo Moretti: 84cla.
La Caravella: 87crb.
La Pedrera: 92bl.
Luigi Bevilacqua: 72bl.
Madera: 100cr.
Palazzo Mocenigo: 90cra.
Muro Venezia S. Stae: 93tr.
Museo della Musica: 74br.
Museo di Storia Naturale: 62bc.
Palazzo Grassi S.p.A : Thomas Mayer 98br.
Peggy Guggenheim Collection: 40–41; Attirement
of the Bride 1940 by Max Ernst © ADAGP, Paris
and DACS, London 2016 40bl; Donna che cammina
(Femme qui marche) (1936) © The Estate of Alberto
Giacometti (Fondation Giacometti, Paris and ADAGP,
Paris), licensed in the UK by ACS and DACS, London
2016 41tr.
Da Rioba: 107cra.
Ristorante Linea d'Ombre: 101br.
Rizzo: 72cr.
Robert Harding Picture Library: age fotostock
Doug Scott 77b; Dr. Wilfried Bahnmuller 20cl; Peter
Barritt 24cla; Neil Emmerson 4cra, 21tl; Lee Frost
4clb; Sabine Lubenow 11cra, 34cla; Harrison Neil
21crb; Massimo Pizzotti 11tr; Roy Rainford 4cl; Tetra
Images 4crb, 18c; Guy Thouvenin 11crb.
Studio Codex Venetia: 106tr.
Tragicomica: 92cl.
Trattoria Alla Maddalena: 121cra.
Venetia Studium: 85tc.
Venturini Souvenirs: 126crb.

Cover

Front and spine – **AWL Images:** Jon Arnold.
Back – **AWL Images:** Jon Arnold bc; **Dreamstime.
com:** Donyanedomam crb, Eriiicristea tr, Luca
Santilli tl, Stevanzz cla.

Pull Out Map Cover

AWL Images: Jon Arnold.

All other images are: © Dorling Kindersley. For
further information see www.dkimages.com.

*As a guide to abbreviations in visitor information
blocks:* **Adm** *= admission charge;* **D** *= dinner;*
L *= lunch.*

MIX
Paper from
responsible sources
FSC™ C018179
www.fsc.org

Penguin
Random
House

Printed and bound in China

First Edition 2002

Published in Great Britain
by Dorling Kindersley Limited
80 Strand, London WC2R 0RL

Published in the United States by
DK US, 1450 Broadway, Suite 801,
New York, NY 10018, USA

Copyright 2002, 2019 © Dorling
Kindersley Limited

A Penguin Random House Company

19 20 21 22 23 10 9 8 7 6 5 4 3 2 1

**Reprinted with revisions 2003, 2005, 2007,
2009, 2011, 2013, 2015, 2016, 2018, 2019**

A CIP catalogue record is available
from the British Library.

A catalogue record for this book is available
from the Library of Congress.

ISSN 1479-344X

ISBN 978 0 2413 6492 5

Phrase Book

In an Emergency

Help!	Aiuto!	eye-yoo-toh
Stop!	Fermate!	fair-mah-teh
Call a doctor.	Chiama un medico	kee-ah-mah oon meh-dee-koh
Call an ambulance.	Chiama un' ambulanza	kee-ah-mah oon am-boo-lan-tsa
Call the police.	Chiama la polizia	kee-ah-mah lah pol-ee-tsee-ah
Call the fire brigade.	Chiama i pompieri	kee-ah-mah ee pom-pee-air-ee

Communication Essentials

Yes/No	Sì/No	see/noh
Please	Per favore	pair fah-vor-eh
Thank you	Grazie	grah-tsee-eh
Excuse me	Mi scusi	mee skoo-zee
Hello	Buon giorno	bwon jor-noh
Goodbye	Arrivederci	ah-ree-veh-dair-chee
Good evening	Buona sera	bwon-ah sair-ah
What?	Quale?	kwah-leh?
When?	Quando?	kwan-doh?
Why?	Perché?	pair-keh?
Where?	Dove?	doh-veh?

Useful Phrases

How are you?	Come sta?	koh-meh stah?
Very well, thank you.	Molto bene, grazie.	moll-toh beh-neh grah-tsee-eh
Pleased to meet you.	Piacere di conoscerla.	pee-ah-chair-eh dee-coh-noh-shair-lah
That's fine.	Va bene.	va beh-neh
Where is/are …?	Dov'è/ Dove sono …?	dov-eh/doveh soh-noh …?
How do I get to …?	Come faccio per arrivare a …?	koh-meh fah choh pair arri-var-eh ah …?
Do you speak English?	Parla inglese?	par-lah een-gleh-zeh?
I don't understand.	Non capisco.	non ka-pee-skoh
I'm sorry.	Mi dispiace.	mee dee-spee-ah-cheh

Shopping

How much does this cost?	Quant'è, per favore?	kwan-teh pair fah-vor-eh?
I would like …	Vorrei …	vor-ray
Do you have …?	Avete …?	ah-veh-teh …?
Do you take credit cards?	Accettate carte di credito?	ah-chet-tah-teh kar-teh dee creh-dee-toh?
What time do you open/ close?	A che ora apre/ chiude?	ah keh or-ah ah-preh/ kee-oo-deh?
this one	questo	kweh-stoh
that one	quello	kwell-oh
expensive	caro	kar-oh
cheap	a buon prezzo	ah bwon pret-soh
size, clothes	la taglia	lah tah-lee-ah
size, shoes	il numero	eel noo-mair-oh
white	bianco	bee-ang-koh
black	nero	neh-roh
red	rosso	ross-oh
yellow	giallo	jal-loh
green	verde	vair-deh
blue	blu	bloo

Types of Shop

bakery	il forno /il panificio	eel forn-oh /eel pan-ee-fee-choh
bank	la banca	lah bang-kah
bookshop	la libreria	lah lee-breh-ree-ah
cake shop	la pasticceria	lah pas-tee-chair-ee-ah
chemist	la farmacia	lah far-mah-chee-ah
delicatessen	la salumeria	lah sah-loo-meh-ree-ah
department store	il grande magazzino	eel gran-deh mag-gad-zee-noh
grocery	la drogheria	lah droh-geh-ree-ah
hairdresser	il parrucchiere	eel par-oo-kee-air-eh
ice cream parlour	la gelateria	lah jel-lah-tair ree-ah
market	il mercato	eel mair-kah-toh
newsstand	l'edicola	leh-dee-koh-lah
post office	l'ufficio postale	loo-fee-choh pos-tah-leh
supermarket	il supermercato	eel su-pair-mair-kah-toh
tobacconist	il tabaccaio	eel tah-bak-eye-oh
travel agency	l'agenzia di viaggi	lah-jen-tsee-ah dee vee-ad-jee

Sightseeing

art gallery	la pinacoteca	lah peena-koh-teh-kah
bus stop	la fermata dell'autobus	lah fair-mah-tah dell ow-toh-booss
church	la chiesa/ la basilica	lah kee-eh-zah lah ah-seel-i-kah
closed for holidays	chiuso per le ferie	kee-oo-zoh pair leh fair-ee-eh
garden	il giardino	eel jar-dee-noh
museum	il museo	eel moo-zeh-oh
railway station	la stazione	lah stah-tsee-oh-neh
tourist information	l'ufficio di turismo	loo-fee-choh dee too-ree-smoh

Staying in a Hotel

Do you have any vacant rooms?	Avete camere libere?	ah-veh-teh kah-mair-eh lee bair-eh?
double room	una camera doppia	oona kah-mair-ah doh-pee-ah
with double bed	con letto matrimoniale	kon let-toh mah-tree-moh-nee-ah-leh
twin room	una camera con due letti	oona kah-mair ah kon doo-eh let-tee
single room	una camera singola	oona kah-mair-ah sing-goh-lah
room with a bath, shower	una camera con bagno, con doccia	oona kah-mair ah kon ban-yoh, kon dot-chah
I have a reservation.	Ho fatto una prenotazione.	oh fat-toh oona preh-noh-tah-tsee-oh-neh

Eating Out

Have you got a table for …?	**Avete una tavola per …?**	ah-veh-teh oona tah-voh-lah pair …?
I'd like to reserve a table.	**Vorrei prenotare una tavola.**	vor-ray preh-no-tar-reh oona tah-voh-lah
breakfast	**colazione**	koh-lah-tsee-oh-neh
lunch	**pranzo**	pran-tsoh
dinner	**cena**	cheh-nah
the bill	**il conto**	eel kon-toh
waitress	**cameriera**	kah-mair-ee-air-ah
waiter	**cameriere**	kah-mair-ee-air-eh
fixed price menu	**il menù a prezzo fisso**	eel meh-noo ah pret-soh fee-soh
dish of the day	**piatto del giorno**	pee-ah-toh dell jor-no
starter	**antipasto**	an-tee-puss-toh
first course	**il primo**	eel pree-moh
main course	**il secondo**	eel seh-kon-doh
vegetables	**i contorni**	ee kon-tor-noh
dessert	**il dolce**	eel doll-cheh
cover charge	**il coperto**	eel koh-pair-toh
wine list	**la lista dei vini**	lah lee-stah day vee-nee
glass	**il bicchiere**	eel bee-kee-air-eh
bottle	**la bottiglia**	lah bot-teel-yah
knife	**il coltello**	eel kol-tell-oh
fork	**la forchetta**	lah for-ket-tah
spoon	**il cucchiaio**	eel koo-kee-eye-oh

Menu Decoder

l'acqua minerale	lah-kwah mee-nair-ah-leh	mineral water
gassata/ naturale	gah-zah-tah/ nah-too-rah-leh	fizzy/ still
agnello	ah-niell-oh	lamb
aglio	al-ee-oh	garlic
al forno	al for-noh	baked
alla griglia	ah-lah greel-yah	grilled
la birra	lah beer-rah	beer
la bistecca	lah bee-stek-kah	steak
il burro	eel boor-oh	butter
il caffè	eel kah-feh	coffee
la carne	la kar-neh	meat
carne di maiale	kar-neh dee mah-yah-leh	pork
la cipolla	la chip-oh-lah	onion
i fagioli	ee fah-joh-lee	beans
il formaggio	eel for-mad-joh	cheese
le fragole	leh frah-goh-leh	strawberries
il fritto misto	eel free-toh mees-toh	mixed fried fish
la frutta	la froot-tah	fruit
frutti di mare	froo-tee dee mah-reh	seafood
i funghi	ee foon-ghee	mushrooms
i gamberi	ee gam-bair-ee	prawns
il gelato	eel jel-lah-toh	ice cream
l'insalata	leen-sah-lah-tah	salad
il latte	eel laht-teh	milk
il manzo	eel man-tsoh	beef
l'olio	loh-lee-oh	oil
il pane	eel pah-neh	bread
le patate	leh pah-tah-teh	potatoes
le patatine fritte	leh pah-tah-teen-eh free-teh	chips
il pepe	eel peh-peh	pepper
il pesce	eel pesh-eh	fish
il pollo	eel poll-oh	chicken
il pomodoro	eel poh-moh-dor-oh	tomato
il prosciutto cotto/crudo	eel pro-shoo-toh kot-toh/ kroo-doh	ham cooked/cured
il riso	eel ree-zoh	rice
il sale	eel sah-leh	salt
la salsiccia	lah sal-see-chah	sausage
succo d'arancia/ di limone	soo-koh dah-ran-chah/ dee lee-moh-neh	orange/lemon juice
il tè	eel teh	tea
la torta	lah tor-tah	cake/tart
l'uovo	loo-oh-voh	egg
vino bianco	vee-noh bee-ang-koh	white wine
vino rosso	vee-noh ross-oh	red wine
le vongole	leh von-goh-leh	clams
lo zucchero	loh zoo-kair-oh	sugar
la zuppa	lah tsoo-pah	soup

Numbers

1	**uno**	oo-noh
2	**due**	doo-eh
3	**tre**	treh
4	**quattro**	kwat-roh
5	**cinque**	ching-kweh
6	**sei**	say-ee
7	**sette**	set-teh
8	**otto**	ot-toh
9	**nove**	noh-veh
10	**dieci**	dee-eh-chee
11	**undici**	oon-dee-chee
12	**dodici**	doh-dee-chee
13	**tredici**	tray-dee-chee
14	**quattordici**	kwat-tor-dee-chee
15	**quindici**	kwin-dee-chee
16	**sedici**	say-dee-chee
17	**diciassette**	dee-chah-set-teh
18	**diciotto**	dee-chot-toh
19	**diciannove**	dee-chah-noh-veh
20	**venti**	ven-tee
30	**trenta**	tren-tah
40	**quaranta**	kwah-ran-tah
50	**cinquanta**	ching-kwan-tah
60	**sessanta**	sess-an-tah
70	**settanta**	set-tan-tah
80	**ottanta**	ot-tan-tah
90	**novanta**	noh-van-tah
100	**cento**	chen-toh
1,000	**mille**	mee-leh
2,000	**duemila**	doo-eh mee-lah
1,000,000	**un milione**	oon meel-yoh-neh

Time

one minute	**un minuto**	oon mee-noo-toh
one hour	**un'ora**	oon or-ah
a day	**un giorno**	oon jor-noh
Monday	**lunedì**	loo-neh-dee
Tuesday	**martedì**	mar-teh-dee
Wednesday	**mercoledì**	mair-koh-leh-dee
Thursday	**giovedì**	joh-veh-dee
Friday	**venerdì**	ven-air-dee
Saturday	**sabato**	sah-bah-toh
Sunday	**domenica**	doh-meh-nee-kah

Index of Main Streets